Jane Addams

Champion of Democracy

BY
Judith Bloom Fradin
AND
Dennis Brindell Fradin

Clarion Books
New York

For our darling granddaughter,
Shalom Amelia Richard,
whose name means "Peace" and "Love"

Clarion Books
a Houghton Mifflin Company imprint
215 Park Avenue South, New York, NY 10003

The text was set in 12.5-point Caslon 3.

www.clarionbooks.com

Printed in the U.S.A.

Library of Congress Cataloging-in-Publication Data

Fradin, Judith Bloom.
Jane Addams : champion of democracy / by Judith Bloom Fradin and
Dennis Brindell Fradin.
p. cm.
Includes bibliographical references and index.
1. Addams, Jane, 1860–1935. 2. Women social workers—United States—
Biography—Juvenile literature. 3. Women social reformers—United States—
Biography—Juvenile literature. I. Fradin, Dennis B. II. Title.
HV28.A35F73 2006
361.92—dc22
[B]
2006011029

ISBN-13: 978-0-618-50436-7
ISBN-10: 0-618-50436-2

RMT 10 9 8 7 6 5 4 3 2 1

ACKNOWLEDGMENTS

The authors thank the following for their gracious and invaluable assistance:

Jim Bade, president of the Cedarville Area Historical Society, for spending two full days sharing the treasures of the society—he was also our "go to" man for a year of e-mailed images and information; Ronald Beam, artist extraordinaire and cofounder of the Cedarville Area Historical Society; Narcissa Engle, vice president of the Cedarville Area Historical Society and our first guide to its many Jane Addams artifacts; Chris Gordy, executive director of the Stephenson County Historical Society—he guided us through his Jane Addams displays and provided us with images for this book; Louise Knight, fellow Evanstonian and Jane Addams biographer, who generously shared chapters of her then-unpublished *Citizen: Jane Addams and the Struggle for Democracy;* Dan Portincaso, facilities manager of the Jane Addams Hull-House Museum, who always had the answers to our most obscure questions; and Mary Pryor, Rockford College archivist, who spent a full day gathering many photos for us.

Contents

Jane Addams in 1892.

Introduction

Today most people either don't know who Jane Addams was or have only a vague idea that she was somehow involved with social work. But her name aroused quite a different reaction a century ago. In the early 1900s, Jane Addams was not only one of the two or three most famous women in the United States, she was one of the most beloved Americans in the world.

Addams first gained fame as the head of Hull House—an institution offering educational, recreational, and other services to needy people—which she and a friend founded in Chicago in 1889. During the nearly fifty years that she ran Hull House, Jane Addams improved life for thousands of Chicagoans, mostly poor and immigrant families. For her achievements at Hull House she was hailed as the "Angel of Democracy," "Miss Kind Heart," the "Lady of God," and even "Saint Jane."

But Jane Addams also dedicated herself to another cause, which stirred up strong feelings both for and against her. She became a pacifist—a person strongly opposed to war. As the head of the Women's International League for Peace and Freedom, she criticized America's entry into World War I (1914–18). Although some people supported her stand, many more were angry at her for speaking out against the United

States' participation in the conflict at a time when American servicemen were dying in Europe.

For her peace efforts she was called "unpatriotic," a "traitor," and even "the most dangerous woman in America." But Jane Addams was utterly convinced that nations could settle their differences with talk rather than with guns, and she remained an outspoken pacifist for the rest of her life. Her decades of dedication to the cause of peace eventually won over many of her detractors, and toward the end of her life she was awarded the Nobel Peace Prize.

In addition to her social work and peace activities, Jane Addams was an accomplished author. She published eleven books and hundreds of articles on such topics as urban poverty, women's voting rights, child labor, and, of course, world peace. And although Miss Addams never married or had children of her own, she played a vital role in the lives of her nieces and nephews, helping to raise several of them.

Perhaps the most remarkable aspect of this remarkable woman was her ability to rise above seemingly insurmountable obstacles. She had terrible back problems and also felt "absolutely at sea" for many years because of severe depression. But Jane Addams overcame these difficulties to become what even her greatest political enemy called "a saint from the skies."

1

Miss Addams, Garbage Inspector

One of Jane Addams's early crusades involved garbage.

Garbage was a huge problem in the cities of the 1800s. It piled up along streets, sidewalks, and alleys, especially in the poorer neighborhoods. Garbage—along with the flies and rodents it attracted—bred disease. This was a major reason half the children born in Chicago in the late 1880s died before reaching their fifth birthday.

Like many other urban areas, Chicago's Nineteenth Ward, where Hull House stood, reeked with the stench of garbage. Back then, Chicagoans piled their trash into wooden boxes that stood beside their houses and apartments. But because collection was irregular, the garbage often overflowed the tops of the boxes, sometimes to the height of one story or more. Hungry animals scattered the trash, turning some locales into virtual garbage dumps.

Neighborhood residents and the Hull House staff complained about the Nineteenth Ward's filthy conditions for several years. One obstacle to progress was that Chicago politicians routinely arranged for their friends to receive the

Chicago's Lake Street, looking east from Clark Street, 1893.
LIBRARY OF CONGRESS

garbage-collection contracts. These men collected the money but were often very casual about actually picking up the garbage.

Jane Addams and her staff protested to City Hall about the unsanitary conditions in the Hull House neighborhood. They filed seven hundred complaints in a single summer, but no one seems to have paid any attention to them. Addams also sent out twelve members of the Hull House Women's Club to investigate conditions in the local alleys. These neighborhood women discovered more than a thousand violations of the city's garbage regulations. The infractions were reported to the health department, but again no action was taken. Miss Addams even installed an incinerator at Hull House to burn some of the debris, but this project didn't make much of a dent in the problem.

Still determined to find a way to clean up her neighborhood, Jane Addams applied to become the Nineteenth Ward's garbage collector in about 1894. She intended to enlist area residents who took part in Hull House programs to help her collect the trash. Chicago officials rejected her bid, but by 1895 Miss Addams had become such a thorn in his side that Mayor George Swift appointed her to another job. She was named Nineteenth Ward Garbage Inspector—the person who made sure that the garbage collectors did their jobs properly.

Every morning at six A.M., Jane Addams walked out the door of Hull House with Miss Amanda Johnson, a young staff member who served as her assistant garbage inspector. The two women climbed into their garbage inspection buggy and told the driver to follow the collection teams that were supposed to pick up the trash around the neighborhood.

Often groups of children ran after the buggy, for they found it amusing to watch the five-foot-three-inch director of Hull House ordering around the brawny garbage collectors. Whenever she saw that they had overlooked a pile of debris or had failed to clean up after the horses that pulled the garbage wagons, Miss Addams would step out of her buggy to speak to the men. She and Miss Johnson followed the garbage wagons on their routes until the end of the day, when the last load of trash was disposed of at a city dump.

Chicago's first female garbage inspector noticed that a number of landlords had failed to provide garbage receptacles. In such cases, she ordered the landlords to install the proper boxes at once, and if they didn't, she took them to court. Finding that the regular crews were not sufficient, she convinced Mayor Swift to provide eight additional crews to assist with garbage collection. Miss Addams also passed out junior cleanup crew badges to three hundred members of the Hull House children's clubs, and had the girls and boys collect old tin cans from the streets and alleys. The cans were sold to a Chicago factory that recycled them, providing a little extra income for Hull House.

Jane Addams served as Nineteenth Ward Garbage Inspector for several months. Then, because she had many other pressing matters to oversee at the settlement house, she turned the post over to her assistant. Miss Amanda Johnson held the post until 1898, when local officials ousted her by ruling that only men could be garbage inspectors.

During the three years that one or the other was on the job, Addams and Johnson made a start toward cleaning up the Nineteenth Ward. In places, pavement was uncovered that no one had seen in years because it had been obscured by layers of debris. Most important, the cleanup lowered the ward's death rate. Recounting this episode in her autobiography *Twenty Years at Hull-House*, Jane Addams wrote:

The careful inspection brought about a great improvement in the cleanliness and comfort of the neighborhood; and one happy day, when the death rate of our ward was found to have dropped from third to seventh [of the city's thirty-four wards] and was so reported to our Women's Club, the applause which followed recorded the genuine sense of participation in the result, and a public spirit which had "made good."

2

Laura Jane Addams, "Ugly Duckling"

Laura Jane Addams was born in a large house in the village of Cedarville, Illinois, on September 6, 1860. She was named for Mrs. Laura Jane Forbes, a Cedarville teacher who had boarded for a time in the Addams home. Laura Jane was the eighth of nine children born to Sarah Weber and John Huy Addams. As was fairly typical in the mid-1800s, only five of the nine Addams children lived past the age of two. Growing up, Laura Jane had an older brother, named John Weber (known as Weber) and three older sisters, Mary Catherine, Martha, and Sarah Alice (called Alice).

Laura Jane's earliest memory was a sad one. In January 1863, Sarah Addams, who had a reputation for her generosity and willingness to help others, received word that a neighbor was about to give birth. The village doctor was out in the country attending to another case. Would Mrs. Addams come and help? Although she was seven months pregnant with her ninth

John Addams.
CEDARVILLE AREA
HISTORICAL SOCIETY

child, Sarah Addams hurried to lend a hand. Shortly after helping to bring a new life into the world, she became ill and had to be assisted back to her home.

On the way, or soon after Sarah Addams arrived home, her baby was stillborn. The doctor came to care for Sarah, who was extremely weak and getting worse. Today's hospitals and doctors probably would have saved her, but in 1863 in a small prairie town there was little the local doctor could do. Day by day Sarah Addams's condition deteriorated as she lay in the same wooden bed where Laura Jane had been born.

Although she was just two years and four months old, Laura Jane sensed that something was terribly wrong. She pounded

Sarah Addams, around 1861.
SWARTHMORE COLLEGE PEACE COLLECTION, JANE ADDAMS COLLECTION

and pounded on the door of her mother's room with her little fists. Finally, she heard her mother say, "Let her in, she is only a baby herself." On January 14, 1863, not long after the little girl visited with her mother for the final time, Sarah Addams recited the Lord's Prayer, took her last breath, and died.

After her mother's death, Laura Jane became very close to her father. John Addams was a man of many talents. Back in 1844, when he and Sarah had come to Cedarville from Pennsylvania, John Addams had begun his career by working as a miller. He soon branched out into other fields besides grinding grain into flour. He served on the Cedarville school board, became the president of the Second National Bank in nearby

This drawing of the Addams homestead appeared in the 1871 Stephenson County record of local property ownership.
CEDARVILLE AREA HISTORICAL SOCIETY

Freeport, raised funds to bring the railroad to northern Illinois, and accumulated the most land of anyone in Stephenson County, in which Cedarville is located. He also was elected to the state senate, where he served for sixteen years, from 1854 to 1870.

Slavery was the major issue that divided the country in the mid-1800s. John Addams despised slavery. For several years before the Civil War began, he turned the family home into a stop on the Underground Railroad—the series of hiding places where escaped slaves were sheltered on their way to freedom. In addition, Addams helped organize a new antislavery party, the Republican Party, in 1854. He became friends with a fellow Republican lawmaker from Illinois, Abraham Lincoln, and supported his successful campaign for president in the election of 1860, held just two months after Laura Jane's birth.

When Laura Jane was a little girl, her father sometimes unlocked a desk drawer and showed her his special treasure— a packet of papers marked "MR. LINCOLN'S LETTERS." Written by Abraham Lincoln while both men were involved in politics, the letters all began "My Dear Double D'ed Addams" and generally were inquiries as to how John Addams planned to vote on issues before the Illinois legislature. There were framed pictures of Lincoln around the Addams house, and by the age of six or seven Laura Jane knew the story of how Mr. Lincoln had worked to free the slaves, guided the nation through the Civil War, and been killed by an assassin just after the war's end in 1865. It made her proud to hold the sixteenth president's letters and to know that her father had been a friend of the great man.

Like other Cedarville children, Laura Jane attended the small village school. But much of her education came right at home. John Addams had an extensive personal collection of books—so large that at one time the Cedarville Library had operated out of the Addams house. Her father made Laura Jane an offer. He would pay her a nickel for each book she read, with one exception. He considered Washington Irving's *Life of Washington* so important that she would receive a quarter for each of its four volumes she read. The little girl began to awaken before dawn to read the books in her father's library. Before handing over the money, John Addams had his daughter tell him about what she had read—what we would call an oral book report.

As Cedarville's wealthiest family, the Addamses were able to take advantage of a recent invention—photography—and so we have photos of young Laura Jane. They show a thin girl whom most people considered pretty but overly serious and sad. Her deep-set, penetrating gray eyes had a somber expression that made her seem more like a miniature adult than a child.

The little girl carried other sorrows in her young heart besides her mother's death. The Civil War, which claimed the most American lives of any war ever fought, had broken out when she was seven months old and had continued until she was about four and a half. John Addams and his friends always seemed to be discussing various battles and the families they knew who had lost fathers, sons, and brothers in the conflict.

Of all the neighbors whose loved ones had died in the war, an elderly couple who lived in an isolated farmhouse made the

deepest impression on Laura Jane. This couple had sent five sons to fight under the Union banner, and by the end of the war in the spring of 1865, all but one of them had been killed. That fall, while hunting wild ducks in the marshes near the little farm, the surviving son was accidentally shot to death, leaving the two old people alone. Jane Addams later wrote in her autobiography: "When we were driven past this forlorn little farm our childish voices always dropped into whisperings as to how the accident could have happened to this remaining son out of all the men in the world—to him who had escaped so many chances of death!"

While still a young child, Laura Jane felt a kinship with unfortunate souls like the elderly couple and began to develop what she later called "a sense of responsibility" toward her fellow human beings. This expressed itself in a recurring nightmare she had at the age of six. In her dream, everyone in town had disappeared and she was standing alone in the village blacksmith's shop. The only way she could save humanity was to make a wagon wheel, but she couldn't because she didn't know how.

Her nightmare seemed so real that she began to visit the blacksmith's shop to learn how to make a wagon wheel. The blacksmith was polite to the oddly serious little girl who was so curious about his work.

"Do you always have to sizzle the iron in water?" she asked, thinking how difficult it would be to handle the hot metal.

"Sure, that makes the iron hard!" replied the burly man in the red shirt.

She would sigh and walk home, "bearing my responsibility as best I could," she later wrote.

There was another reason for the sad look in the little girl's eyes. In early childhood she had suffered an illness believed to have been tuberculosis of the spine. Laura Jane recovered, but she was left with a curved back, which caused her to stand crookedly and walk in a pigeon-toed manner. No matter how often she was complimented for her lovely face, Laura Jane was convinced that she was hideous—an "ugly duckling," she later wrote. She was so ashamed of her appearance that she developed the habit of remaining out of sight in the presence of strangers. For example, out-of-town visitors sometimes attended the Sunday school class taught by John Addams. On those occasions Laura Jane would walk out of the church apart from her father the moment class ended. She later explained why:

> I imagined that strangers were filled with admiration for this dignified person, and I prayed with all my heart that the ugly, pigeon-toed little girl, whose crooked back obliged her to walk with her head held very much upon one side, would never be pointed out to these visitors as the daughter of this fine man. I simply could not endure the thought that "strange people" should know that my handsome father owned this homely little girl.

John Addams sensed his daughter's feelings. One day when the family was visiting Freeport, Laura Jane approached the bank where her father was president just as he came out. She was about to turn and head the other way, but before she could flee, her father lifted his tall silk hat and made an impressive bow to her. Seeing her father do that in front of so many townspeople convinced Laura Jane that he was proud to be seen with her. It also cured her of hiding when strangers were around her family.

Soon there would be another reason for her spirits to be lifted.

3

"Jennie and Georgie"

With their mother gone, Laura Jane's oldest sister, Mary, who was fifteen years older, took charge of the household. Mary was especially needed to care for Laura Jane when their father was in Springfield, the state capital, on legislative business. The Addams household also included Polly Bear, an elderly nursemaid who many years earlier had been Sarah Addams's childhood nurse. Although Laura Jane loved Mary and Polly, nothing could make up for the loss of her mother.

In November 1868, nearly six years after his wife's death, John Addams remarried. His second wife was Anna Haldeman, a widow from nearby Freeport with two sons. Eight-year-old Laura Jane became attached to her stepmother from the start. The two of them shared a love of books. Anna insisted that Laura Jane, who had never done anything athletic, ride with her on horseback through the countryside. Anna also brought a piano with her and filled the big Addams house in Cedarville with music. Soon Laura Jane was calling her stepmother "Ma," and Anna was treating her like one of her own children.

Jennie's father and her stepmother, Anna Haldeman Addams, 1868.
SWARTHMORE COLLEGE PEACE COLLECTION, JANE ADDAMS COLLECTION

Harry Haldeman, Anna's older son, was eighteen when his mother married John Addams. Harry later became a doctor and married Laura Jane's next older sibling, Alice, who was seven years older than she was. Anna's other son, George, was just nine months younger than Laura Jane, and she and Georgie soon became inseparable playmates and best friends. We should no longer call her Laura Jane, though, for around this time she decided to be known as Jennie, a variation of her middle name.

Jennie and Georgie had adjoining rooms on the second floor of their home. All day they attended school together. When the dismissal bell was rung, they ran home to play with their yellow dog, Ponto, and with the pet chickens their parents had given them. In the wintertime they ice-skated on the frozen pond behind their house, and in the summer months they had picnics and went boating and swimming.

Jennie was so busy having fun with Georgie that she forgot about her deformed back and her "ugly duckling" complex. Cedar Creek, with a fifty-foot-tall cliff behind it, flowed alongside the Addams home. Lighting their way with candles, Georgie and Jennie explored the caves along the cliff. They searched the nearby woods and hills for snakes, which they carried on sticks to a secret hiding place. Together they collected fossils and unusual rocks.

Some of their activities were dangerous. Their parents would have been furious had they known what Jennie and Georgie did at John Addams's sawmill. The two children would sit on moving logs and then, just before they reached the saw, jump off. The goal was to see who could come the closest to the sharp-toothed saw before leaping to safety.

Drawing of the Addams mill in Cedarville.
RONALD BEAM, CEDARVILLE AREA HISTORICAL SOCIETY

Another of their exploits nearly ended in disaster. Georgie decided that, with Jennie's help, he would lower himself down the side of the cliff to investigate an owl's nest. First they tied one end of a rope around Georgie's waist. Then they tied the other end around a maple tree at the top of the cliff. As an extra precaution, Jennie was also to hold on to the rope.

"Don't let go, Jennie!" said Georgie, for if the rope slipped off the tree, only she could keep him from falling onto the rocks below.

With Jennie tightly holding the rope, Georgie lowered him-

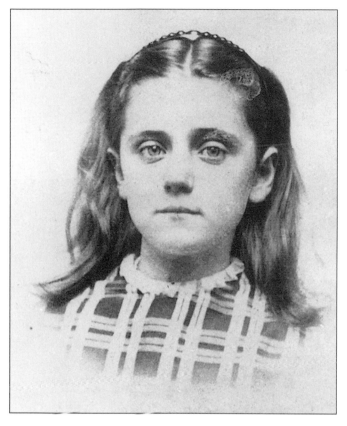

Eight-year-old Jennie.
SWARTHMORE COLLEGE
PEACE COLLECTION,
JANE ADDAMS COLLECTION

self down the rocky ledges, inching toward the tree where the owl lived. Suddenly, a chunk of the cliff broke away beneath Georgie's feet, and the next instant the rope ripped away from the maple tree and through Jennie's hands. Her stepbrother plunged downward. Jennie hurried to the cliff's edge, afraid of what she would see on the rocks below. By incredible good fortune, Georgie had landed in the branches of the owl's tree. Although he was badly bruised and Jennie's hands were bleeding from rope burns, they both made it home safely.

Now and then the Addamses went on vacations. When Jennie was about ten years old, she, Georgie, and their parents made a seventy-five-mile journey in the family carriage to Madi-

Eight-year-old Georgie.

son, the capital of Wisconsin. Jennie's father explained that they were going to see a very special bird: an eagle that had been the mascot of a company of Wisconsin soldiers during the Civil War. Named Old Abe for President Lincoln, the eagle had fought in thirty-eight battles with the Wisconsin troops, screaming as he flew over the enemies' heads. Although the bird had some feathers shot out, Old Abe survived the war and afterward was given a home in the basement of the Wisconsin state capitol. Old Abe made a deep impression on Jennie. She and Georgie both drew detailed pictures of the trip, and forty years later Jane Addams wrote that seeing the eagle inspired her with a desire to do something "heroic" with her life.

Jennie and her stepbrother both loved to draw. They made cards identifying themselves as artists and spent many rainy days sketching. They also amused themselves by asking each other riddles, including the following, which are from a joke book Jennie owned called *Pepper and Salt:*

QUESTION: What is the Smallest Room in the world?
ANSWER: The Mush-room.

Q: What Animals are in the Clouds?
A: Rain—Dear.

Q: What is the most Ancient Furniture?
A: The Multiplication Table.

Q: If you were to throw a White Stone into the Red Sea, what would it become?
A: Wet.

Q: What is that which, although only four inches long and three inches wide, contains a solid foot?
A: A Shoe.

Q: Why can't the Devil Skate?
A: How in H-ll can he?

Q: What never asks questions, but requires
frequent answers?
A: The front door Bell.

Q: What two Letters express the most agreeable
people in the world?
A: U and I.

Jennie and Georgie attended this school, which was built five years before Jennie was born.
CEDARVILLE AREA HISTORICAL SOCIETY

*Cedarville school, circa 1870. Jennie, holding a hat, is the second
girl from the left. Georgie is the middle boy sitting on the grass.*
ROCKFORD COLLEGE, HOWARD COLMAN LIBRARY ARCHIVES

By 1871, eleven-year-old Jennie and her stepbrother were
the only two children still at home. Anna's older son, Harry,
had completed his medical studies and was working as a doctor in a town near Cedarville. Jennie's sister Martha had died
at the age of only sixteen in a typhoid fever epidemic. Mary, the
oldest Addams child, had married John Linn, the minister of a
Cedarville church. Alice was a student at Rockford Female
Seminary, a school thirty miles from Cedarville that later
became Rockford College. Weber, Jennie's only male sibling,
had moved out of the house and was living on his own.

The Addams and Haldeman children all kept in touch by

writing letters. For example, in August 1871, Mary sent Alice a letter explaining how Jennie's friendship with George had done wonders for their little sister's spirits. "Jennie and Georgie never seem to be quite as contented as when they are alone, without any company," Mary wrote Alice. A few months later, Jennie wrote to her sister Alice to inform her about events at home:

> Cedarville Ill.
> January 14, 1872
>
> My dear sister,
>   Georgie received your letter and as it is my turn to answer I will do so now. Ma came home on Friday. We did not expect her till Saturday. I went in yesterday to have my teeth filled, but he [the dentist] found that [nothing] needed filling. A man fell off of the court house last week and was killed. I had my hair up in [rollers] last night and I couldn't get to sleep for ever so long, but they curled nicely this morning. All send love.
>   from Jennie

As Jennie and Georgie grew older, Anna introduced them to the plays of William Shakespeare, which the youngsters read aloud, acting out the various parts. They learned to play chess, a game that occupied many of their winter evenings. A diary she kept in 1875 reveals that by the age of fourteen Jennie was a lively girl with many interests and several friends besides George:

Jennie's oldest sister, Mary.
SWARTHMORE COLLEGE
PEACE COLLECTION,
JANE ADDAMS COLLECTION

Saturday, January 9, 1875

This morning it is so cold Pa did not go to town. In the forenoon George and I drew and painted pictures. I mended my purple dress. We did not go to singing [lessons] as it was too cold. But Ma, George, and I played chess.

Monday, April 12, 1875

This morning went to school. Although it is pretty wet we played ball and Mat Graham knocked and lost the ball and so we had to stop. I intended to take a horseback ride this evening but it began to rain and so I couldn't. Edward Mitchell and I played croquet.

Friday, April 23, 1875

This morning just as we were finishing
breakfast we saw a wagon coming with jingling
bells on the mules and a young fellow came in
and said he had brought the [new] piano. It is
as beautiful as can be. This evening we learned
[to dance] the polka.

Thursday, April 29, 1875

Today we spelled at school. We first had a
match and George, Alma, Meda, and I stood
Mat Graham, Ceda Jackson, Mary Smith,
and Charles and beat them too. We then had a
spelldown and I [missed] the word "paralysis."

Her stepbrother also sparked Jennie's ambitions. Georgie
planned to attend college and become either a scientist or a
physician like his older brother, Harry. If Georgie was going to
college, Jennie reasoned, why shouldn't she? While it was true
that few girls attended college in those years, more schools
were opening their doors to females all the time. In 1841,
Oberlin College in Ohio had become the first American college
to grant degrees to both sexes. All-female colleges were being
founded, too, such as Vassar in New York in 1861 and Smith
in Massachusetts in 1871.

At college she might study to become a doctor or a scientist
like Georgie. Or, since she had a flair for writing, perhaps she

Jane practiced writing her name on the first pages of her diary.
CEDARVILLE AREA HISTORICAL SOCIETY

would become an author like Louisa May Alcott, whose novel *Little Women* she had read over and over. By then, young Jennie also thought about working with the poor.

The idea came to her one day while she and her father were on a trip to Freeport. They were driving their buggy through an impoverished neighborhood where the tumble-

Sixteen-year-old Jennie . . .

down shanties were built on pilings of wood to protect them from river flooding. Shocked by the sight, Jennie asked, "Why do people live in such horrid little houses so close together?"

After her father had explained that there were many poor people in the world, she declared: "When I grow up, I will have a large house, but it will not be built among the other large houses, but right in the midst of horrid little houses like those." Because she grew up to do what she said, some people think that the story is just a legend made up at a later time. How-

. . . and sixteen-year-old Georgie.

ever, a Cedarville schoolteacher insisted that the story was true, because he personally heard it from John Addams.

In any case, by her teens Jennie began to discuss her future with her father. Her dream was to attend Smith College. John Addams could easily afford the tuition, and she had earned outstanding grades at public school in Cedarville, so she probably would have been admitted there. But to Jennie's dismay, despite her father's keen interest in education, he absolutely refused to send her to Smith or to any other eastern college. Instead, he insisted that she attend nearby Rockford Female

Seminary, even though it wasn't yet an official degree-granting college.

For one of the few times in her life, Jennie argued with her father. Why couldn't she go to Smith or Vassar like other bright girls? He countered that her sisters Mary and Alice had both studied at Rockford Female Seminary, and it had been good enough for them. Perhaps, like most nineteenth-century fathers, John Addams believed that a woman's place was in the home, and that an outstanding education was wasted on young women. But it seems more likely that, having lost five of his and Sarah's nine children, he simply couldn't bear the thought of his youngest daughter going so far from home.

In the fall of 1877, after nearly a decade of being almost constantly together, Jennie and Georgie went their separate ways. He traveled thirty-five miles from Cedarville to attend all-male Beloit College in Wisconsin. Jennie packed her bags and traveled thirty miles from home to enroll at Rockford Female Seminary.

4

Jane Addams, College Graduate

Jennie, who had never lived away from home for a prolonged period, was terrified when she first arrived at Rockford Female Seminary. Her classmate Eleanor Frothingham Haworth later recalled meeting Jennie as they both hurried to take the written examinations required of new students at the school:

> On Saturday, September 22, 1877, on my way to a room in Middle Hall, I met a little girl with very pretty light-brown hair, pushed back, and particularly direct, earnest eyes. She looked as I know I was feeling, very trembly inside. She said her name was Laura Jane Addams and she had just come from Cedarville. The examiner had no mercy on us. She gave us a regular "teachers' examination," full of very difficult questions. But we pulled through. I have always wondered if I looked as young and worried as Jane did that day.

The frightened "little girl with very pretty light-brown hair" made a change upon entering the school. Formally named Laura Jane and then called Jennie, she now wanted to be known by her middle name. She remained Jane Addams for the rest of her life, and is known by that name to this day.

Anna Peck Sill had started the seminary nearly thirty years earlier and, at the age of sixty-one, was still its headmistress when Jane Addams arrived. Unlike a college such as Smith, which maintained the same lofty scholastic standards as a good men's college, Rockford Female Seminary combined religious training with academics. The seminary's purpose, Miss Sill wrote in the school catalogue, was to "develop moral and religious character in accordance with right principles, that it may send out cultivated Christian women in the various fields of usefulness." Miss Sill's ultimate goal was to convince her students to become missionaries, so that they would spread the Christian Gospel throughout the world. By the time Jane Addams entered the school, at least thirty-seven seminary graduates were serving as foreign missionaries, while dozens more were married to missionaries or ministers.

The seminary schedule was rigorous. Jane had to awaken every morning at five in order to be ready for breakfast by seven. No one could be seated in the dining room until Miss Sill gave a signal, and at every table a faculty supervisor monitored the young ladies' behavior. Each day Jane and her classmates were required to attend chapel and observe the evening "silent hour" set aside for prayer. On Sundays they had to attend church in the morning and Sunday school in the afternoon. In addition, there was a monthly "fast day" devoted to prayer,

Anna Peck Sill.

ROCKFORD COLLEGE, HOWARD COLMAN LIBRARY ARCHIVES

during which the students weren't allowed to eat, and a "prayer week" every January.

Anna Peck Sill ruled the seminary with an iron hand. It was said that whenever one young woman heard her coming, she hid in a closet—and *she* was a teacher. New students were asked a riddle: "Why is the Rockford Female Seminary like a new house?" The answer: "Because it has a *firm Sill*." Miss Sill punished students who broke the rules, and any girl who left the school grounds without permission or who was found guilty of other serious transgressions faced expulsion.

Despite the strict rules, Jane flourished at the seminary. In fact, it could be said that while Georgie had helped his stepsister emerge from her shell, the seminary began transforming the girl who had considered herself an "ugly duckling" into a swan. Her nephew James Weber Linn, who later wrote a biography called *Jane Addams,* described her as a student at the seminary:

> When Jane entered Rockford, she was no longer "homely," if indeed she ever had been except in her own eyes. She was small, five feet three inches tall, and weighing ninety-five pounds—but she no longer "carried her head on one side," only a little forward, which with her seeking eyes gave her an appearance of unusual earnestness. Throughout her years in the institution, she sparkled with enthusiasm. In the town of Winnebago, eight miles from Rockford, they still tell stories of the lively young girl who came from the college to visit her

sister [Mary, the mother of James Weber Linn]. There was a wedding at a farmhouse some miles from Winnebago one snowy evening, at which her brother-in-law was to officiate. Jane insisted on driving out with him in the sleigh, which tipped over twice in the drifts. At the farmhouse Jane burst into the kitchen, shook the snow from her skirts, and cried, "I can't wait to tell the girls I've been to a wedding and turned over twice to get there!"

To provide the students with a little entertainment, Miss Sill arranged for the young men of Beloit College, twenty-five miles away, to make group visits to Rockford Female Seminary on Saturdays. The young women and men weren't allowed to be alone together, so teachers supervised their hayrides, picnics, and sleigh rides. Jane enjoyed these visits, which gave her the opportunity to see her stepbrother Georgie.

Jane became friends with another Beloit student, Rollin Salisbury. On January 15, 1881, Rollin wrote to Jane, inviting her to a lecture, "The Wonder of Growth in Animals," and the other letters they exchanged don't hint at any romance between them. However, James Weber Linn later revealed that Salisbury, who became a noted University of Chicago geography professor, wanted to marry Jane. She turned him down, as she would her other suitor from Beloit College.

Since they weren't blood relatives, Jane and her stepbrother Georgie could have married without violating any laws or customs. Jane's sister Alice had already married Georgie's older brother, Harry. Moreover, Anna Haldeman Addams very much wanted Jane to marry her younger son. The problem was that while Georgie had begun to feel romantic toward Jane, she loved him solely as a dear brother and friend. Georgie's romantic interest in her disturbed Jane and would soon cause problems in their family.

Jane formed many lasting friendships at the seminary. Eleanor Frothingham Haworth, the girl who met Jane on the way to the written examinations, became her close friend. So did Sarah Anderson, a woman in her thirties who was the school accountant as well as a gymnastics teacher. But her best friend at the seminary was Ellen Gates Starr, a student from Durand, Illinois, who was intensely interested in religion and art. Ellen remained at the seminary for a year, then became a schoolteacher, settling in Chicago. When apart, Jane and Ellen exchanged twenty-page letters, and during vacations Ellen visited Jane at the Addams home in Cedarville.

Her classmates marveled at Jane's independent spirit and willingness to challenge authority. One day, while teaching a literature class, Miss Sill discussed the Spanish novel *Don Quixote* and pronounced it "Don *Quix*-utt." Up shot the hand of Jane Addams, who explained that the novel's title should be pronounced "Don Kih-*hoh*-tee." Although either pronunciation is acceptable, the students sided with Jane, which wasn't so bad, but they also laughed at Miss Sill, who suspended the entire class for two days for their impolite behavior. At chapel exercises the day of this incident, Jane wrote a defiant poem on a page of her friend Eleanor's hymn book:

Eighteen-year-old Jane Addams.

CEDARVILLE AREA
HISTORICAL SOCIETY

Life's a burden, bear it.
Life's a duty, dare it.
Life's a thorn crown, wear it,
And spurn to be a coward!

Not only Miss Sill but the other faculty members tried to persuade the students to become missionaries. A teacher even spoke to Jane about it during the silent hour, an evening period when no one was permitted to speak except on matters of urgency. She did not intend to spend her life spreading Christianity in remote parts of the world, insisted Jane, who resented being pressured. If she became a missionary, it would be *her* choice—not because Miss Sill and the teachers talked her into it.

In a notebook she kept during the 1878–79 school year, Jane Addams inscribed her personal motto: "Always do what you are afraid to do." Because she seemed so brave to them, the girls asked her to serve as a go-between whenever they had conflicts with Miss Sill or another faculty member. As further evidence of their confidence in her, Jane's schoolmates elected her class president each of her four years at the seminary.

Jane was also the ringleader of a few girls who dared to break the school rules. Late at night they would gather in her room in defiance of the bedtime curfew. Their activities seem harmless by today's standards, but they would have caused the girls trouble had they been caught. Jane and her friends placed a blanket over a slit in the door to hide the light coming from her room, then ate popcorn and cashew nuts that they had smuggled in, while reading aloud such forbidden romantic plays as William Shakespeare's *Romeo and Juliet*.

In her autobiography, Jane Addams confessed to something far more serious than the midnight popcorn parties. On one occasion she and four friends decided to experiment with drugs. They crushed some pills made of opium—a powerful and addictive drug—and then ate them. The girls became very ill and passed out on the floor of one of their rooms. A teacher who found the girls revived them and gave them a medication that made them vomit. Fortunately, all five girls recovered. The teacher did not tell Miss Sill, who might have expelled the girls had she known what they had done.

Although rebellious and occasionally foolish, Jane was a superb student. During her four years at the seminary she maintained a grade average of 9.862 out of a possible 10, or what we would call an A+. She achieved this despite taking more difficult courses than most of her classmates. While Jane was a student there, the seminary was in the process of becoming a certified women's college. In hope of qualifying for a college degree once the change occurred, Jane registered for six or seven of the most demanding classes the school offered each semester. During her four years at the seminary she studied Latin, Greek, German, Bible history, botany, astronomy, chemistry, algebra, geometry, Shakespeare, music, and several other subjects.

Discovering that she had a talent for speaking, Jane joined the seminary's Debating Society. Her senior year she was the only woman to compete in an oratorical competition organized by the leading colleges in Illinois. She also wrote for the *Rockford Seminary Magazine*, serving as its editor her senior year. In July 1879 the magazine published her article "Follow Thou Thy Star," in which she declared that everyone has a "life-purpose," but that most of us "throw it away" because we lack the nerve to follow our "true inner nature." In another article

Jane Addams (holding the parasol) and some of her Rockford Female Seminary classmates. Eleanor Frothingham Haworth, who later became a missionary in Japan, is standing on the far left.

ROCKFORD COLLEGE, HOWARD COLMAN LIBRARY ARCHIVES

she advised her classmates: "Do what you believe in doing! Keep one main idea, and you will never be lost."

Jane was named valedictorian of her class. Her family watched as she graduated on June 22, 1881, in the school chapel. Speaking in front of a giant number 81—for Class of 1881—spelled out in white and red flowers, Jane spoke of her classmates' potential to do great things:

> We stand united today in a belief in beauty,
> genius, and courage, and that these can
> transform the world!

Jane and the sixteen other graduates received diplomas but not a college degree. A year later, Jane Addams was informed that the seminary had at last become Rockford College, a degree-granting institution. Since she had taken sufficient classes, she was invited to receive her college degree at the 1882 graduation.

As she walked up to the podium to accept her college diploma, Jane Addams may have thought about the changes that had occurred in her life since she had spoken of transforming the world a year earlier.

5

"Absolutely at Sea"

When she graduated from Rockford Female Seminary in 1881, Jane Addams faced a question that young people still wrestle with upon completion of their schooling: What will I do with the rest of my life? While today many avenues are open to both men and women, in the 1880s most young women were expected to marry and start raising children. Except for teaching, nursing, missionary work, and—in the cities—doing factory or domestic labor, women had few job opportunities.

Medicine was then a growing field for women in the United States, which by 1880 had 2,400 female physicians. Deciding that she wanted to become a doctor, Jane asked her father if he would send her to the University of Edinburgh in Scotland, which had opened its medical school to women in 1869. Once again he refused, because he couldn't stand the idea of his daughter going thousands of miles from home for several years. However, he did offer to send her on a European tour before she settled down.

Jane spent the first few weeks of the summer of 1881 at

home in Cedarville with her father and stepmother. She was a few months shy of her twenty-first birthday, and with her plans to study medicine thwarted, Jane had no idea what she wanted to do with her life. She felt terribly depressed and had begun to suffer from frequent backaches and colds. At the seminary she had been quite healthy and energetic despite her busy schedule. Now she had little to do except write letters to her friends and read, and yet she felt constantly tired. The fact was, the girl who had advised her classmates, "Keep one main idea, and you will never be lost," was completely adrift.

In early July, Jane and her family were indirectly involved in a tragic event. Flora Guiteau, a young woman whose father was head cashier at John Addams's bank in Freeport, was one of Jane's best friends. The Guiteau family, including Flora's mentally disturbed half brother, Charles, had often been guests at the Addams home. On July 2, 1881, Charles Guiteau shot President James Garfield at a Washington, D.C., railroad station. The president lived seventy-eight days before dying of his wounds.

Journalists descended on the Freeport-Cedarville area to dig up information about the assassin and his friends and family. Americans were so enraged by the shooting that everyone associated with the Guiteaus became a target of abuse. Nearly all her friends abandoned Flora, but Jane Addams remained steadfast and even sat with her when Charles was hanged.

In August, John Addams decided to take his wife and youngest daughter away from the unwanted attention they were receiving in connection with President Garfield's shooting. Mr. Addams wanted to investigate some copper-mining

Jane's best friend from college, Ellen Gates Starr, in 1880.

SWARTHMORE COLLEGE
PEACE COLLECTION,
JANE ADDAMS COLLECTION

land in Michigan's Upper Peninsula. Viewing this as an opportunity to provide them with a change of scenery, he took Anna and Jane along.

Jane's father was exploring a mining property near Marquette, Michigan, when he suddenly complained of terrible stomach pains. Realizing that he was seriously ill, Jane and her stepmother tried to rush him home, but on the way his condition worsened. They checked him into a hospital in Green Bay, Wisconsin. John Addams died, apparently of a ruptured appendix, in Green Bay on August 17, 1881.

Jane was numb with grief. She wrote to Ellen Gates Starr, asking her friend to spend a day or two with her in Cedarville.

"The greatest sorrow that can ever come to me has passed," she told Ellen. "I will not write of myself or how purposeless and without ambition I am, only prepare so you won't be disappointed in me when you come."

By the terms of his will, John Addams left Jane nearly sixty thousand dollars—equal to more than a million dollars in today's money. She still had her heart set on becoming a physician, so she applied to the Women's Medical College of Philadelphia, which had opened in 1850 as the world's first medical school for women. She was accepted, and in the fall she moved to Philadelphia to begin her medical studies.

Jane's stepmother accompanied her. Anna wanted to be with Jane, and they both had another reason to go to Philadelphia. Anna's son Dr. Harry Haldeman and his wife—Jane's sister Alice—were temporarily living there. Jane, Anna, Harry, and Alice moved into a home together on the edge of downtown Philadelphia.

Jane had little time to spare for her family. Monday through Friday she attended lectures and demonstrations from eight in the morning until six at night, and on Saturday there was a half day of classes. She was devastated to find that medicine didn't interest her. She had trouble concentrating on her studies. To make things worse, the dean of the medical college constantly tried to persuade the students to become medical missionaries in China or India. It was a little like dealing with Miss Sill all over again—only this time Jane was in no mood to argue.

She broke down completely in the spring of 1882. Severe back pain left her continually exhausted. In the grip of a physi-

Jane's sister Alice Addams Haldeman and Dr. Harry Haldeman.
SWARTHMORE COLLEGE PEACE COLLECTION, JANE ADDAMS COLLECTION

cal and nervous collapse, Jane withdrew from school and admitted herself to the Mitchell Hospital of Orthopedic and Nervous Diseases. This Philadelphia clinic specialized in treating high-strung young women who had suffered nervous breakdowns.

The Mitchell Hospital administered a "rest cure"—six weeks of doing little except resting in bed. No visitors were allowed, so Jane couldn't even see family members. Books, newspapers, and writing materials were forbidden, so she couldn't read or communicate with anyone by letter. Besides bed rest, the only therapies to relieve her depression and back pains were a diet of milk and other dairy products, and daily massages and electric shock treatments.

To use a nineteenth-century term, the Mitchell Hospital's methods were largely "humbug." Jane Addams realized this herself and several years later wrote: "To be put to bed and fed on milk is not what [a patient] requires. What she needs is simple, health-giving activity, which involves the use of all faculties."

After six weeks Jane Addams did leave the clinic feeling different: a lot worse. She couldn't know it at the time, but she was at the beginning of an eight-year period that would be marked by poor health and depression. She wrote in her autobiography: "From the time I left Rockford in the summer of 1881 until Hull-House was opened in the autumn of 1889 . . . during most of that time I was absolutely at sea."

Anna and Jane took the train back to Cedarville in mid-1882. Jane's back pain was now worse than ever, and it seemed that everything else was going wrong. Jane's brother, Weber, had taken their father's death even harder than she had. Now living with his wife and daughter in a new house atop the bluff near the family homestead, Weber had a severe mental collapse. He began to hear voices and suffer bouts of depression worse than any Jane had experienced. Weber became so unmanageable that he would be in and out of mental institutions for the rest of his life.

On top of that, Jane's stepbrother George was also battling depression. Convinced that her younger son and stepdaughter would both come out of the doldrums if they married, Anna became upset with Jane once it became clear that she had no intention of marrying George.

Amidst all these family crises, Jane felt that if she could only get her back better, she would be on the road to recovery. Alice Haldeman and her husband had moved to Mitchellville, Iowa, where Dr. Haldeman opened a medical practice. In September 1882, just a few months after Jane had returned to Rockford College to be awarded her college diploma, Dr. Haldeman offered to operate on his stepsister in hope of correcting her spinal curvature. The procedure was new and might not work, he explained, but by this time Jane was ready to try anything.

In the early winter she went by train to Mitchellville, where her brother-in-law performed successful surgery on her back. Her nephew James Weber Linn later explained that following the operation, Jane received some bad news from Dr. Haldeman: She would never be able to have children.

Her recovery was slow, and for another two months she had to stay in bed at Harry and Alice's home. Jane and her sister entertained themselves by taking turns reading aloud Mary Shelley's novel *Frankenstein* and other books. Just before returning to Cedarville in early 1883, Jane wrote to her friend Ellen Gates Starr: "I have had the kindest care and am emerging with a straight back and a fresh hold on life I hope."

Jane's back felt better, but the question still remained: What would she do with her life? In the 1800s, young people from wealthy families often made what was called a "grand tour" of Europe before they married or began a career. On such tours they typically studied the languages of countries they visited, made pilgrimages to landmarks and museums, and kept jour-

On tour in London. Clockwise from left: Harriet, Jane, Mary,
Sarah, Anna, and Mrs. Young.
ELLWOOD HOUSE AND MUSEUM, DEKALB, ILLINOIS

nals describing everything they saw. With no other prospects in view, Jane Addams decided to embark on a two-year tour through about a dozen countries. She assembled a group of traveling companions consisting of her stepmother, Anna; her cousin Sarah Hostetter; her seminary classmate Mary Ellwood; Mary's sister Harriet; and the Ellwood girls' aunt, Mrs. Young.

Jane spent the early summer of 1883 reading travel guides

and planning their itinerary. Several days after the Fourth of July, she and Anna left Cedarville. On the way to New York they stopped in Chicago, where Jane was fitted with a back brace made of steel, whalebone, and leather that Dr. Halde-man had prescribed. Although it was heavy and irritated her skin, the brace helped her back feel even better.

The group assembled in New York City, and on August 22, 1883, they boarded the *Servia,* then one of the world's largest ocean liners. From the deck of the ship Jane waved to her stepbrother George, who had come to wish them *bon voyage.* The *Servia* left the pier, and as it moved past the Brooklyn Bridge, Jane burst into tears. Her sadness at leaving her home-land didn't last long, however. Once out at sea, the young woman began to look forward to what she might encounter on the other side of the Atlantic.

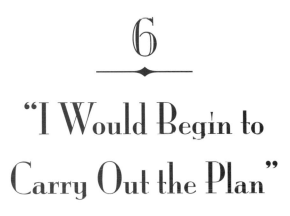

6

"I Would Begin to Carry Out the Plan"

Jane Addams and her companions stepped ashore in Ireland on August 29, 1883, after an ocean crossing of only one week. Soon after their arrival, Jane's mental and physical condition dramatically improved—perhaps because for the first time in years she had no responsibilities. Her back felt so good that she took off the brace and never wore it again.

Jane was excited to actually see places she had only read about in books. In Ireland they toured Blarney Castle and spent three weeks in Dublin. In England they visited William Shakespeare's home and toured Windsor Castle, the residence of Britain's Queen Victoria. They climbed mountains and rode horseback in Switzerland, attended the opera and saw famed actress Sarah Bernhardt perform in France, and viewed the works of Michelangelo and other great artists in Italy. They also toured Scotland, Wales, the Netherlands, Germany, Austria, and Greece. During the summer of 1884, George Haldeman met them in Europe and joined them for a few weeks of sightseeing.

One event that made a strong impression on Jane had nothing to do with beautiful scenery or historic old buildings. On a Saturday night in London, Jane and a group of other tourists made an excursion by carriage into the poverty-stricken East End. Saturday night was when London street vendors auctioned off their decaying fruits and vegetables to the poor people who lived in that area. In her autobiography, Jane Addams described how, from the safety of the carriage, she watched the poor, hungry people trying to buy the spoiled food to fend off starvation:

> On a Saturday night, I saw for the first time the overcrowded quarters of a great city at midnight. From the top of an omnibus [large carriage] which paused at the end of a dingy street lighted by occasional flares of gas, we saw two huge masses of ill-clad people clamoring around two hucksters' carts. They were bidding their farthings and ha-pennies [quarter pennies and halfpennies] for a vegetable held up by the auctioneer, which he at last scornfully flung to the successful bidder. One man had bid on a cabbage, and when it struck his hand, he instantly sat down on the curb, tore it with his teeth, and devoured it, unwashed and uncooked as it was. They were huddled into ill-fitting, cast-off clothing. Their pale faces were dominated by the cunning of the bargain-hunter who starves if he cannot make a successful trade,

Gustav Doré's rendering of a poor section of London, 1872.

JERROLD BLANCHARD AND GUSTAV DORÉ, FROM *LONDON: A PILGRIMAGE*
(LONDON: GRANT & CO., 1872).

[as they] clutched forward for food which was
already unfit to eat.

In the days that followed, Jane related, she went about London "afraid to look down narrow streets and alleys lest they
disclose again this hideous human need and suffering." Yet,
she added, "during the following two years on the continent, I
was irresistibly drawn to the poorer sections of each city." She
wished she could do something about the poverty that she wit-
nessed: But what?

Jane was so disturbed by something she saw in Germany
that she *did* do something about it. On a snowy winter morning
she was looking out her hotel window when she noticed, as she
later wrote:

> Crossing and recrossing [the town square] a
> single line of women with heavy wooden tanks
> fastened upon their backs. They were carrying to
> a cooling room these tanks filled with a hot brew
> incident to one stage of beer making. The women
> were bent forward under the weight which they
> were bearing. Their faces and hands, reddened in
> the cold morning air, showed clearly the white
> scars where they had previously been scalded by
> the hot stuff which splashed if they stumbled ever
> so little on their way.

She could see, across the square, the brewery that employed
the women. So furious that she didn't stop to consider whether

it was her place to interfere, she rushed downstairs, crossed the square, and entered the brewery, where she demanded to speak to the owner. He agreed to see the American woman, but once he learned the reason for her visit, he refused to discuss his laborers' working conditions with her.

As the novelty of seeing strange places wore off, Jane found herself thinking once again about what she would do with her life. "I have lost confidence in myself, and have improved in nothing," she wrote to her friend Ellen Gates Starr.

Jane Addams, 1885.
ROCKFORD COLLEGE,
HOWARD COLMAN
LIBRARY ARCHIVES

Only one stop remained on their itinerary—Spain—when Jane and her stepmother received a message from home. Jane's oldest sister, Mary, was expecting her fifth child but was ill. Jane was needed back home to help care for her sister and her family. Cutting their grand tour a little short, Jane and Anna departed from Liverpool, England, on May 30, 1885, once again aboard the *Servia*. After a year and nine months abroad, they arrived in New York in early June and immediately took the train back to Cedarville.

For the next two and a half years, Jane had little opportunity to think about herself. She was too busy caring for others. For long periods on and off she helped care for her sister Mary's children in the Illinois towns of Harvard and then Geneseo. She and Anna also spent prolonged periods in Baltimore, where George was studying biology at Johns Hopkins University. Intent on keeping an eye on her younger son, Anna rented an apartment in Baltimore, where she and Jane ate their meals with George. By now, George realized that Jane would never have anything but sisterly feelings toward him, and he expressed his hurt feelings by acting cold and distant toward her.

Meanwhile, Jane had finally found something that she enjoyed. She volunteered at a Baltimore nursing home for elderly African American women several days a week and discovered that it made her feel useful. "I had such a pleasant afternoon yesterday with the old women in the Colored Shelter," she wrote to her sister Alice in late 1886. "They are so responsive and know me well enough now to be perfectly free." She found the experience so rewarding that she also vol-

Alice and Harry's daughter, Marcet Haldeman, was born in 1887.

ROCKFORD COLLEGE,
HOWARD COLMAN LIBRARY
ARCHIVES

unteered at an orphanage for African American girls. Her friend Ellen Gates Starr later said that Jane's volunteer work in Baltimore helped inspire the founding of Hull House.

In late 1887, George dropped out of Johns Hopkins and went back to Cedarville with his mother. Jane then decided to return to Europe—this time not just to sightsee. She wanted to visit Toynbee Hall in London's East End, the impoverished area she had toured on her first European trip.

Founded in 1884, Toynbee Hall was the world's first "settlement house"—an institution that provides educational and social services for the needy. Toynbee Hall began a new approach to aiding the poor, who had traditionally depended on the charity of wealthy people. The principles behind Toynbee Hall were that those who could afford it should help the poor out of a spirit of brotherhood, and that the best kind of aid was to teach the needy to help themselves.

Toynbee Hall was called a "settlement house" because its staff of young male college graduates "settled," or lived, there. These young men were called "residents," and the neighborhood people came to them for classes ranging from reading and writing to history and literature. The residents also scheduled concerts and art exhibits for the neighborhood people, and they began a program that sent needy children to summer camp in the country.

Jane Addams set sail from Hoboken, New Jersey, on December 14, 1887, with Sarah Anderson, her teacher friend from the seminary. The two women arrived in England just before Christmas. Soon afterward, they were joined by Ellen Gates Starr, who had come to collect European artworks for the Chicago school where she taught. Jane and her two friends toured Europe for the next six months. According to Jane, the idea of what she should do with her life came to her during this trip—in an unlikely place.

In April 1888, Jane attended a bullfight in Madrid, Spain. As she watched the bloody spectacle, it occurred to her that she should establish a settlement house in a poor section of Chicago, a booming city in her home state. She would model it after Toynbee Hall, except that the residents would be young women rather than young men.

Why the idea came to her at the bullfight she never could explain, but, she later wrote, she was so excited that "I made up my mind that the next day, I would begin to carry out the plan, if only by talking about it . . . to Miss Starr. I even dared hope that she might join in carrying out the plan." Ellen greeted Jane's idea enthusiastically and promised to assist her.

Two months later, in June 1888, Jane visited Toynbee Hall. Not only did it live up to her expectations, but she found some kindred spirits four thousand miles from home. Several of the residents confessed to feeling lost after college graduation—a feeling that lasted until they came to work at Toynbee Hall.

Soon after her visit to the world's first settlement house, Jane sailed for America. As she crossed the ocean, Jane Addams was, for the first time in seven years, eager to move on with her life.

7

"The Shelter We Together Build"

In January 1889, having first seen to some family and financial matters, Jane Addams traveled by train to Chicago, where she met Ellen Gates Starr. The two friends began to search for a house in a neighborhood where a settlement would do the most good, or, as Jane had once said to her father, "a large house" amidst "little houses."

Jane couldn't have picked a better place than Chicago to carry out her plan. First permanently settled by Jean Baptiste Pointe Du Sable, a black man who arrived in 1779, Chicago grew slowly and by 1835 had only 3,200 residents.

The following year, Illinois Supreme Court Judge Theophilus Smith made a speech celebrating the start of a Chicago canal project. Standing on a barrel, Judge Smith declared that Chicago would have 20,000 residents in twenty years and 50,000 in fifty years. As the crowd jeered at his predictions about the muddy little prairie town, someone sarcastically asked how many people Chicago would have a century into the future, in 1936. "A hundred years from this time you will have a city of one hundred thousand!" Judge Smith answered. This sounded so preposterous that several rowdy men in the crowd pulled the judge off the barrel and splashed water in his face.

Judge Smith was wrong, for he grossly underestimated Chicago's growth. Strategically located on Lake Michigan and linked to the Mississippi River by the completion of the Illinois and Michigan Canal in 1848, Chicago became a boomtown. By 1860 the city had 110,000 residents—more than Judge Smith had said it would have in 1936. When Jane Addams arrived in 1889, Chicago's population had soared to one million, making it the nation's second-largest city after New York.

Chicago wasn't just a leader in population. As early as the 1860s, more railroad lines met in Chicago than in any other city on earth. A wide array of products went in and out of the city by train and boat, but Chicago was known for four industries in particular. It was a world leader in the meatpacking, lumber, grain, and mail-order businesses.

Partly because much of the city had been built of wood, Chicago suffered a catastrophic fire in 1871, eighteen years before Jane Addams's arrival. The Great Chicago Fire killed three hundred people, destroyed thousands of houses and other structures, and left one hundred thousand Chicagoans homeless. Chicago would die, pessimists predicted, but Chicagoans rebuilt their city, often using brick and other fireproof materials. After the Great Fire, Chicagoans began constructing a new kind of building—the skyscraper. Visitors came from afar to marvel at the ten-story Home Insurance Building, completed in 1885 as the first metal-frame skyscraper in the world.

A lithograph of the Great Chicago Fire of 1871.

Chicago offered every kind of entertainment a person might seek. In 1885, one hundred thousand people attended the Chicago Opera Festival. Art lovers flocked to the Art Institute. Chicago was home to America's most successful baseball team, the Chicago White Stockings (today the Chicago Cubs), winners of six National League pennants between 1876 and 1886. The city also featured numerous theaters, music and dance halls, beer gardens, and vaudeville shows.

Visitors often saw just one side of Chicago—the lovely lakefront, the fabulous mansions of the wealthy merchants, the majestic skyscrapers, and the glittering night spots. But there was another side to the city: some of the worst slums in the nation.

There were entire neighborhoods where the residents lived packed together in filthy tenements and shacks. Many poor Chicagoans had no heat in the wintertime, no running water,

State and Madison streets, after the Great Fire.
LIBRARY OF CONGRESS

and no neighborhood schools. Because the opportunity to bathe was rare for the poor, dirt sometimes accumulated on children until their skin resembled scales. In addition, the milk delivered to poor families was often spoiled.

These unsanitary conditions claimed a large toll, particularly among the very young. In the city as a whole, half the children born in 1889 wouldn't live to celebrate their fifth birthdays. The death toll was even higher in poor neighborhoods, where families might have ten children in the hope that three or four would reach adulthood. Adults also suffered from outbreaks of disease, which included smallpox, cholera, scarlet fever, tuberculosis, typhoid fever, and dysentery. In 1885, for example, epidemics killed approximately one hundred thousand Chicagoans, or about one in every eight of the city's population. In 1890, just a year after Jane Addams arrived, a typhoid fever epidemic swept Chicago and continued for two years. During this period, Chicago had the highest death rate from this disease of any major American or European city.

Poor Chicagoans who managed to survive the epidemics worked at the lowest-paying and most difficult jobs—if they found work at all. Thousands of men worked in filthy conditions at the Union Stockyards: slaughtering livestock, cutting the meat, and cleaning up the remains of the animals. Other men were garbage collectors, dockhands, and maintenance and construction workers.

Impoverished women worked as laundresses, servants, seamstresses, and scrubwomen, also for low wages. Thousands more worked in sweatshops—factories and shops where women made clothing in unhealthy surroundings. Because

Chicago's Union Stockyards, 1905.
LIBRARY OF CONGRESS

they were paid according to the number of garments they completed, the women worked almost around the clock, pausing only for a few hours to eat and sleep, and often bringing their young children to assist them. For this drudgery the hourly pay for the women amounted to about seven cents, while their children earned about four cents.

Many needy Chicago women became prostitutes. Chicago was so widely known as a place where men could find prostitutes that in 1889 a guidebook appeared describing the city's nine hundred brothels. Much as Jane Addams had been shocked by the squalor of London's East End, a journalist from London was astonished by the matter-of-fact way that Chicagoans accepted prostitution. Chicago "makes a more amazingly open display of evil than any other city known to me," he wrote. Besides prostitution, poor neighborhoods were plagued by gambling halls, drug dens, and thieves.

There were two main reasons for Chicago's widespread poverty. First, the city had many corrupt politicians who were more concerned with lining their own pockets than with improving conditions for the poor. In the late 1800s, Chicagoans seeking a building permit or a tax adjustment often had to pay bribes to their aldermen and other politicians. It was also common for the men who ran the city to sell their votes to the highest bidder.

Chicagoans had a name for political corruption. They called it *boodling* and referred to dishonest politicians as *boodlers*. The man known as "the Prince of the Boodlers" was Johnny ("De Pow") Powers, who ran the Nineteenth Ward. On his alderman's salary of twelve dollars a month, Powers managed to own two saloons, several gambling halls, and a large home. That was possible because, as chairman of the committee that decided who would do business with the city, he was in a perfect position to accept bribes and kickbacks, which he did—as much as $50,000 from a single individual.

There was another reason for the large number of poor people in Chicago. As of 1889, three out of every four Chicagoans had either been born outside the United States or were the children of foreign-born parents. The city had large numbers of immigrants from Ireland, Italy, Greece, Poland, Germany, Norway, Sweden, Denmark, and Russia. Since many newcomers entered Chicago with a meager knowledge of English, little money, few belongings, and no job prospects, it was inevitable that the neighborhoods where they settled would suffer from poverty.

Upon Jane's arrival in Chicago in early 1889, she and Ellen Gates Starr moved into a boarding house together. Each day they hired a carriage to take them around the city as they searched for a place to establish their settlement. Although her inheritance provided Jane with a yearly income of about $3,000 (equal to about $60,000 today), Ellen was no longer teaching, so they needed donors to help them carry out what they called their "scheme." While making their rounds, the two friends approached wealthy society women for donations, and

Home sweatshop workers in a New York tenement, 1913.

they sought out charity workers to ask their advice. They also met with young women who had recently graduated from college, for once they began their settlement, they would need to assemble a staff.

Her efforts to get the scheme rolling completed a change in Jane Addams that had begun with her European trips. The depressed semi-invalid of a few years earlier had vanished, replaced by an energetic young woman with a purpose in life. Occasional bouts of depression would trouble her for many years to come, but she would always be able to deal with them. The winter ended, however, and Jane and Ellen hadn't yet found a place to establish their settlement.

One Sunday afternoon early in the spring of 1889, the two friends were out exploring when they noticed what Jane later called "a fine old house" at the corner of Halsted and Polk streets. Over the next several days, they did some investigating. The mansion was in an area of mostly foreign-born working poor people belonging to about thirty ethnic groups. Among them were Italians, Irish, Germans, Bohemians (people from an old kingdom in what is now the Czech Republic), Greeks, French Canadians, and Polish and Russian Jews.

If ever a section of Chicago needed a settlement house, this was it. The house was in the Nineteenth Ward, one of the most impoverished and neglected of Chicago's thirty-four wards. Typically, area residents lived crammed together in rickety shacks with no running water or indoor toilets. Uncollected garbage piled up everywhere, and as a result of these filthy conditions, the ward had one of the city's highest death rates. There were several parochial schools in the ward but few pub-

Children playing leapfrog in a garbage-strewn alley in the Hull House neighborhood, around 1900.

UNIVERSITY OF ILLINOIS, JANE ADDAMS MEMORIAL COLLECTION

lic schools. Boys and girls as young as nine or ten spent their days working in the area's sweatshops and factories. For many of the children the only form of amusement was hunting for rats in the muddy streets.

The "fine old house" Jane and Ellen had passed had been built in 1856 by Charles J. Hull, a wealthy real-estate developer. After Hull had moved out in the late 1860s, his mansion, which was one of the few neighborhood buildings to survive the Great Chicago Fire, had been rented out as an old people's home, a used-furniture store, and a firm that manufactured school desks. Hull had died shortly before Jane Addams and Ellen Gates Starr discovered the house. His cousin Helen Culver, a former teacher and high school principal, had inherited his estate, which included many buildings as well as four million dollars.

Jane and Ellen made an appointment to speak to Miss Culver, who pleasantly surprised them by expressing interest in aiding the poor. She had founded a school for former slaves in the South, she explained, and had done volunteer work at a night school for boys who worked during the day. Miss Culver agreed to rent a large portion of the house to them at a yearly rate of about seven hundred dollars. But Miss Culver thought so highly of their project that she soon changed her mind and gave Jane Addams the entire house for nothing. In gratitude, they named their settlement Hull House, in honor of Miss Culver's cousin Charles J. Hull.

Before moving into Hull House, Jane and Ellen returned to their respective homes in Cedarville and Durand, Illinois, to spend a few weeks with their families. Jane's homecoming was an ordeal, for George's mental state had deteriorated. About a year earlier he had been found wandering in confusion through Iowa, more than a hundred miles from home. For the time being George was living in the Cedarville house with his mother, but he had become uncommunicative. Anna blamed George's condition on Jane. Had Jane married him, Anna believed, her son would have fulfilled his dream of becoming a doctor or a scientist and would be living happily. Jane was relieved to leave Cedarville in August and go back to Chicago, which would be her home for the rest of her life.

For about a month Jane and Ellen worked at fixing up Hull House, furnishing it and hiring workmen to make much-needed repairs. Jane spent about five thousand dollars getting

Hull House into shape—a sizable chunk of her inheritance. Then, on Wednesday, September 18, 1889, twelve days after her twenty-ninth birthday, Jane Addams moved into Hull House with Ellen Gates Starr and a housekeeper named Mary Keyser, who had formerly worked for Jane's family in Cedarville.

In a poem she wrote several years later, Jane Addams expressed her hopes for the settlement house that she would direct for nearly half a century:

> A house stands on a busy street
> Its doors are opened wide,
> To all who come it bids good cheer,
> To some it says, Abide.
> Gathered within its friendly walls
> A club of women find
> The joys of glad companionship,
> Contentment for the mind.
> For they have learned what all must learn,
> That in life's hardest storm,
> The shelter we together build
> Is all that keeps us warm;
> That fellowship is heaven-sent,
> That it alone can free
> The human heart from bitterness,
> And give it liberty.
> Some hours they dream with civic pride
> Of cities that shall be,
> Within whose streets each citizen
> Shall live life worthily.

8

"A Sense of Fellowship"

As Jane Addams wrote in her poem, the door of Hull House *was* "opened wide" on the September night in 1889 when she, Ellen, and Mary Keyser first slept there. They were so excited to be actually living in Hull House that they neglected to close a side door. It showed the "honesty and kindliness of our new neighbors" that no one tried to enter the mansion through the open door during the night, declared Jane. She then decided to keep the doors unlocked day and night so that the neighborhood people would know they were always welcome.

The first Hull House "visitors" didn't come into the house. As Jane, Ellen, and Mary finished breakfast their first morning in Hull House, they heard the clink of breaking glass. A group of young boys, evidently trying to frighten or catch a glimpse of the women inside, had been throwing stones at the house, and had broken a parlor window. Jane was neither angry nor disturbed but considered the incident proof that children will find trouble if they have nothing else to do.

Over the next few days, many neighborhood people—sometimes entire families—came by to find out about Hull House.

The first event Jane planned was what she called a "reading party." She sent invitations to the Italian immigrant women of the neighborhood announcing that on a certain day Miss Starr, who knew the language, would begin reading a novel aloud in Italian. The reading party was so successful that Jane arranged to have Ellen and others read aloud and discuss more books. Besides literature, Ellen also began teaching classes in art history.

Gradually, Jane Addams assembled a staff who lived at Hull House as well as volunteers who came and went. The first person to join Jane and Ellen as a Hull House resident was Anna Farnsworth, who was put in charge of the Girls' Gymnastics Club and the Fairy Story Club for children. Hull House had been open only a few days when Jane Addams began Chicago's first kindergarten there, placing a young woman named Jenny Dow in charge. The kindergarten started with about twenty-five children and was so popular that it soon had a waiting list of seventy girls and boys.

One day Jenny Dow brought her tall, blond friend Mary Rozet Smith to Hull House. Mary came from an extremely wealthy family, but because of severe asthma she had spent much of her time traveling for her health instead of attending college. At the age of twenty-one she was searching for something meaningful to do. Not long after they met, Jane Addams sent Mary a note inviting her to "share our destiny" at Hull House. Miss Smith joined the staff, heading both the Girls' Club and the Boys' Club and helping to establish the Hull House Music School. Mary Rozet Smith and Jane Addams were to become lifelong friends.

Two early Hull House residents later became very famous in their own right. Julia Lathrop joined the Hull House staff as a resident in 1890 and remained there for more than twenty years. Julia and Jane had similar backgrounds. Born in Rockford, Illinois, in 1858, Julia was just two years older than Jane. Like Jane, she attended Rockford Female Seminary, and her father served in the Illinois legislature. Soon after arriving at Hull House, she began making "friendly visits"—meetings with neighborhood people to tell them about the settlement house and learn about their needs. Julia also taught English literature and ran the Plato Club, a group for elderly men who discussed vari-

Julia Lathrop, who later became the first Chief of the United States Children's Bureau.

LIBRARY OF CONGRESS

Florence Kelley spearheaded the effort to end child labor in the United States.
LIBRARY OF CONGRESS

ous philosophies of life on Sunday afternoons. Julia later became the first Chief of the United States Children's Bureau.

Florence Kelley was the other early Hull House resident who became a prominent reformer. The thirty-two-year-old Kelley was more suited for the rough-and-tumble world of Chicago politics than anyone else at Hull House. The daughter of Philadelphia politician William "Pig Iron" Kelley, Florence had been one of the first female graduates of Cornell University and afterward earned an economics degree from the University of Zurich in Switzerland. She had married a physician, with whom she had three children.

The marriage was unhappy, though, so she brought her children to Illinois, where she planned to obtain a divorce and start a new life. In Chicago she heard about the new settlement house at 335 South Halsted Street. Kelley later described how she arrived at Hull House unannounced:

> On a snowy morning between Christmas 1891 and New Year's 1892, I arrived at Hull-House, Chicago, a little before breakfast time, and found there Henry Standing Bear, a Kickapoo Indian, waiting for the [unlocked] front door to be opened. It was Miss Addams who opened it, holding on her left arm a pudgy baby belonging to the cook, who was [preparing] breakfast. Miss Addams was hindered in her movements by a super-energetic kindergarten child, left by her mother while she went to a sweatshop [to work].
>
> We were welcomed as though we had been invited. We stayed, Henry Standing Bear as [a handyman] several months; and I as a resident seven happy, active years.

Jane Addams arranged for Florence Kelley's children to live with friends in the Chicago suburbs. At Hull House, Florence trained immigrant women for jobs. She earned a law degree while based at Hull House, and later became one of the foremost leaders in the fight for legislation to protect child and adult laborers.

The number of Hull House residents rose rapidly, from six to fifteen, then twenty. Jane Addams soon decided that excluding men from the staff was a mistake. In 1890, George Hooker became one of Hull House's first male residents. He was assigned to investigate garbage collection in the neighborhood, which led to Jane Addams becoming Nineteenth Ward Garbage Inspector a few years later. The male residents boarded in homes near Hull House until separate housing was built for them in 1896.

Jane Addams had a gift for coordinating large numbers of women and men and assigning them jobs that best suited them. If a few neighbors (as the Hull House staff called the neighborhood people) expressed interest in establishing a class or a club, Jane found someone to run it. Starting in the afternoon and extending until about nine o'clock at night, Hull House offered activities for people of all ages. Neighbors could take classes to learn English, German, and French. Classes were offered in child care, cooking, drawing, singing, piano, athletics, chemistry, and mathematics. In addition, there were storytelling hours, youth clubs, and reading groups.

Jane hadn't forgotten the stone throwers who appeared that first morning at Hull House. For boys she formed the Young Citizens' Club, which combined gymnastics with citizenship lessons; the Hull House Columbian Guards, which mixed marching drills with neighborhood cleanup projects; and the Debating Club, which taught boys to fight with words instead of fists. Not content to be just an administrator, Jane led some reading parties and ran the Pansy Club, a social club for girls.

Her willingness to listen and learn from others was another of Jane Addams's traits that helped Hull House succeed. The resi-

Child labor was still a problem in 1911, when more than two million American children were working—many of them twelve hours or more a day, six days a week.
LIBRARY OF CONGRESS

dents were much like a large family. The women routinely addressed each other as "sister" (although they often called Jane Addams "J.A.") and talked late into the night about ways to better serve the community. Florence Kelley, for example, felt that Hull House should lead the fight for legislation to help the needy. As a result of Sister Kelley's arguments, J.A. became more politically astute.

In the early 1890s, Florence Kelley, Julia Lathrop, and Jane

Addams pressured Illinois legislators to pass a law protecting women and children who worked in factories. This resulted in the Illinois Factory Act of 1893, which improved workplace conditions, limited the workday for women factory employees to eight hours, and ordered that no child under fourteen be allowed to work at manufacturing.

Jane Addams astonished her colleagues with her boundless energy and her enormous capacity for work. Her nephew and biographer, James Weber Linn, later reported that J.A. typically worked fourteen and sometimes sixteen hours a day. If she wasn't arranging for a lecturer or a new resident to come to Hull House, she was starting a club for working girls. If she wasn't talking to a neighbor, she was off on a speaking tour or meeting with wealthy people to raise funds. Two of the biggest contributors to Hull House became her close friends.

Louise deKoven Bowen, a banker's wife who sometimes accompanied J.A. on her speaking tours, was the largest single donor to Hull House. Between 1893, when she joined the Hull House Women's Club, and 1953, when she died, Mrs. Bowen contributed nearly three quarters of a million dollars to the settlement, plus a seventy-two-acre tract of land in Waukegan, Illinois, that was made into a summer camp for Hull House children.

Helen Culver also became friends with Jane Addams and sometimes went bicycling with her. In addition to the Hull House mansion, Miss Culver turned over other neighborhood properties she owned for J.A.'s use.

These donations helped the settlement grow into a complex consisting of several structures. Around 1891, J.A. took pos-

Louise deKoven Bowen.
UNIVERSITY OF ILLINOIS,
JANE ADDAMS MEMORIAL
COLLECTION

session of a saloon that stood next to Hull House. She converted it into the Hull House Diet Kitchen, which provided soups, porridges, and other inexpensive but nutritious foods to sick and impoverished neighbors.

Since many local families had no running water at home, J.A. installed bathrooms and laundry tubs for their use at the rear of the mansion. Because many young children had no place to stay while their parents went to work, J.A. opened a day nursery (what we would call a day-care center) known as the Children's House. During the 1890s, J.A. also established a boarding house for working women in a building near the Hull House mansion. Rent was inexpensive, and women who lost their jobs could draw on an emergency fund at the boarding house, which was called the Jane Club.

"Jane," her friend Ellen Gates Starr once remarked, "if the Devil himself came riding down Halsted Street, you'd say, 'What a beautiful curve his tail has.'" Her gift for finding the

Children playing at Hull House, around the turn of the twentieth century.
UNIVERSITY OF ILLINOIS, JANE ADDAMS MEMORIAL COLLECTION

good in everyone proved useful in her dealings with William Kent, a young man who owned a string of rundown tenement houses and stables near Hull House. Rather than confronting Kent for being a slum landlord, J.A. tried convincing him to change his ways, even taking him on a tour of his own property to show him its deplorable condition. She was so persuasive that he agreed to tear down the dilapidated structures and turn the land over to her. In 1894, she converted it into Chicago's first public playground for children.

With a donor's help, Jane Addams purchased a horse stable near the Hull mansion. She transformed it into the Butler Art Gallery, which displayed paintings provided by the Art Institute of Chicago and local art collectors. The Chicago Public Library opened a branch in the Butler Art Gallery. The number of readers grew so large that in 1894 the Hull House Library moved to a separate storefront building.

The Hull House neighbors had artistic talents that had gone untapped until J.A. arrived on the scene. By the early 1890s, she had opened the Hull House Art Studio, headed for fifty-one years by resident Enella Benedict. Classes were taught in the studio building, which also provided working space for artists. The Hull House Music School was located in yet another building. There, children learned to compose and play music. The Boys' Club Brass Band was one of the most popular—and probably the noisiest of the groups connected with the Music School.

Many European-born neighbors of Hull House possessed ancient crafts skills that were being replaced by modern machinery, J.A. realized. She established the Hull House

This young girl is glazing a small clay bowl in a Hull House workshop.
CEDARVILLE AREA
HISTORICAL SOCIETY

Labor Museum in a building near the mansion. It featured neighborhood people who gave demonstrations in pottery and basket making, spinning and weaving, wood- and metalworking, and other crafts. The demonstrators taught visitors their crafts, but that wasn't all they achieved. American-born children tended to be ashamed of their parents' and grandparents' old-country ways. Shame turned to pride when the young people saw that their relatives were popular attractions in a museum!

Hull House became especially well known for theater. Plays were first presented in a large room at the Hull mansion and later in a gymnasium. But the plays attracted such large audi-

Plays in various languages were presented at Hull House to entertain neighborhood residents.

UNIVERSITY OF ILLINOIS, JANE ADDAMS MEMORIAL COLLECTION

ences that people had to be turned away, so Louise deKoven Bowen provided money to build Bowen Hall, a 750-seat auditorium. The plays were presented not only in English but sometimes in Polish, Greek, Russian, Italian, and other languages, so that non-English speakers could enjoy them. When not being used for plays, Bowen Hall hosted dances, parties, and lectures.

By the early 1900s, Hull House had grown to thirteen buildings and was home to about forty staff residents, a quarter of them men. Among the residents were physicians, attorneys, journalists, businessmen, teachers, scientists, musicians, and artists. The Hull House settlement had become a vital part of the neighborhood. Of the 70,000 people who lived within six blocks of Hull House around the turn of the century, roughly 9,000 participated in the settlement's programs in any given week.

Organizing all the programs and dealing with so many people was much like running a city. But J.A. thrived on the work and was happier than she had been in many years. For what could be more satisfying than establishing what Jane Addams called "a sense of fellowship" with thousands of her neighbors?

9

"Miss Kind Heart"

Despite her long hours at Hull House, Jane Addams found time for family matters. In the early 1890s, her oldest sister, Mary, became ill with cancer. Mary's husband, the Reverend John Linn, was struggling to earn a living, so Jane dipped into her inheritance to provide her sister with medical care. She had Mary admitted to a hospital in Kenosha, Wisconsin, paid her medical bills, and often took the train from Chicago to visit her.

In the summer of 1894, Mary's condition worsened. Jane was summoned to her sister's bedside and saw that the end was at hand. Mary Addams Linn slipped into a coma and died on July 6, 1894, at the age of forty-nine.

Jane had adored her oldest sister, who had helped raise her following their mother's death. The Reverend Linn wasn't able to care for the four surviving children his wife had left behind, so Jane stepped in, just as Mary had done for her many years earlier.

The children ranged in age from eleven to twenty-two. At the time of his mother's death, the oldest child, John Linn Jr.,

86

was attending a seminary in Chicago. His aunt Jane provided funds so that he could continue his education. J.A. took the other three children—eighteen-year-old James Weber, fourteen-year-old Esther, and eleven-year-old Stanley—to Hull House, where they lived with her for a time while she planned for their future.

J.A. sent James Weber to the University of Chicago. He frequently visited his aunt and later wrote a biography of her. Jane enrolled her niece Esther in a school near Cedarville and later rushed to her aid when she was expelled from Rockford College. J.A. especially wanted to keep a close eye on Stanley, whose health was poor. She sent him to a Chicago school and later to a boarding school. Stanley probably spent more time at Hull House than the other three children, sleeping in a room next to J.A.'s second-floor bedroom during his visits. Stanley was staying with his aunt when a burglar—or rather a *would-be* burglar—entered the house.

Late one night, J.A. was startled by a noise in her bedroom. She awoke to find a man searching for something valuable to steal. Worried that the intruder would terrify her Stanley, who was sleeping in the next room, Jane Addams commanded, "Don't make a noise!"

The surprised intruder ran toward the window through which he had entered.

"You'll be hurt if you go out that way!" J.A. warned. "Go down by the stairs and let yourself out." The man took her advice and departed without taking anything.

James Weber Linn, who recounted this story, also described another occasion when his aunt awoke to find an intruder in

Hull House around 1890.
STEPHENSON COUNTY HISTORICAL SOCIETY

her room. J.A. spoke to the man and learned that he wasn't a professional burglar but an out-of-work neighbor who was desperate for money. J.A. told him to leave but to come back at nine o'clock in the morning, when she would try to find him employment. He did as instructed, and she soon found him a job.

Spurred on by Florence Kelley, J.A. stepped up her involvement in politics. In 1895, she took charge of cleaning up the neighborhood when she became the Nineteenth Ward Garbage Inspector. Around that time she decided to oust Johnny "De Pow" Powers as political boss of the Nineteenth Ward.

Despite being "the Prince of the Boodlers," Alderman Powers was extremely popular in his ward. He managed this by funneling some of the illegal kickbacks and bribes he received back into the neighborhood. Another of his nicknames was "the Great Mourner," because he attended about a dozen funerals a week, providing flowers and private carriages for grieving relatives. This meant a great deal to poor families, who felt that their loved ones should "go out in style," even though they may have lived in poverty.

Johnny Powers (center) and his crowd.

If a Nineteenth Ward resident landed in jail, Powers would bail him out, then "fix" the case with the judge. Powers also bragged that he had arranged for 2,600 Nineteenth Ward residents to be placed on the Chicago city payroll. At Christmastime, Powers passed out thousands of free turkeys to the poor.

At first, Alderman Powers tried to befriend Jane Addams. Whenever he saw her, he would smile and call her "a saint from the skies." Before Christmas 1893, he came to Hull House offering to provide hundreds of turkeys for her to distribute to needy neighbors. The offer was discussed at the weekly Hull House staff meeting. J.A. and everyone else decided to have nothing to do with Powers.

Many neighborhood people couldn't understand what Miss Addams had against their generous alderman. She explained that he gave them little gifts while keeping most of the money he stole for himself. Worse still, he deprived them of truly important things, like schools and clean streets. His practice of getting accused criminals out of trouble was also harmful, for it kept the thugs in the neighborhood. As for being "the Great Mourner," all those funerals might not be needed if he worked to provide the services people deserved. But most people in the ward were so beaten down and impoverished that they were grateful for Johnny Powers's handouts.

One particular incident spurred J.A. to take on Johnny Powers. On Taylor Street a school was housed in a dangerous, decaying building that wasn't big enough to hold all the students who wanted to enroll. J.A. and her staff spoke to Chicago school board members and were in the process of convincing them that a new school building was needed when "De Pow" stepped in. Since the pupils at the Taylor Street school were the children of immigrants who couldn't vote, he had no interest in building a new school for them. Instead, he arranged for a new parochial school to be built. Jane Addams had nothing against a new Catholic school, but what was needed more was a school that would be available to all children, whether Protestant, Catholic, Jewish, or of any other faith.

At that time, each of Chicago's thirty-four wards had two aldermen. Powers, who was considered unbeatable, was one of the Nineteenth Ward aldermen, while the other was generally a crony of his. In 1895, Jane Addams and some of her colleagues convinced Frank Lawler, a resident who was a leader of the Hull House Men's Club, to run for the ward's second aldermanic seat. Lawler beat out three other candidates and took his place alongside Powers in the Chicago City Council. Reportedly, the new alderman was bribed by Powers and became one of his supporters, but Lawler couldn't defend himself against the charges because he died soon after his election.

In the midst of her struggle with Johnny Powers, J.A. began feeling seriously ill for the first time since she'd moved to Hull House. She was suffering from appendicitis—the condition that had killed her father fourteen years earlier. Either because Jane was too ill to be moved or because she refused to go to the hospital, a surgeon came to Hull House with his instruments, three assistants, and a portable operating table. On September 10, 1895, four days after her thirty-fifth birthday, J.A. was put to sleep with ether and the surgeon operated on her diseased appendix. She survived the procedure, and by about Christmastime, after several months of recuperation, she was ready to resume her Hull House duties as well as her battle with Johnny Powers.

Jane decided to attempt the near impossible: defeat Powers in his own reelection bid. For the Hull House candidate J.A. chose another Men's Club member, William Gleeson. An Irish immigrant who had risen to become president of the Chicago Bricklayers' Union, Gleeson was a man to whom the poor people of the Nineteenth Ward could relate. Chicago newspapers followed the campaign closely, for there was something appealing about the young female do-gooder from a small Illinois town trying to unseat one of Chicago's most powerful political bosses.

It was said that Powers was so worried about losing that he spent $20,000 in the campaign's last days to bribe voters, toss coins to their children, and pass out free kegs of beer at the saloons. On Election Day—April 7, 1896—gangs of Powers's henchmen threw rocks at and beat up Gleeson supporters. Had women been permitted to cast ballots, Gleeson might have won, but like most of the nation, Chicago didn't allow females to vote, and so Johnny Powers triumphed by a count of 4,064 to 2,703.

In 1898, Alderman Powers pulled some strings and had Hull House resident Amanda Johnson removed as Garbage Inspector in favor of one of his cronies. More determined than ever to defeat him, Addams and her colleagues chose Simeon Armstrong to oppose Powers in the 1898 election.

By now Addams and Powers were bitter enemies. The director of Hull House traveled around the ward raising money for Armstrong, who had worked as a laborer before completing night school and becoming a lawyer. J.A. also spoke to newspapers and gave talks about Powers's "boodling." Her speeches were published in several journals, and people as far away as Europe read about the political war being waged in Chicago.

Powers lashed back at the woman he had once called "a saint from the skies." Newspapers quoted him as saying, "The trouble with Miss Addams is that she is jealous of my charitable work in the ward. Hull House will be driven from the ward." Powers predicted to the *Chicago Record* newspaper that "a year from now there will be no such institution" as Hull House.

Friends of Johnny Powers sent Addams insulting messages. In January 1898, she received an anonymous letter from a man who ripped into her for becoming involved in "man's work":

> Jane Addams
>
> As a voter and citizen of the 19th ward, and interested in the welfare of this great and beautiful city, I have watched, and noted with interest, how for the past few years, you have worked and sought the defeat of that good, noble, and charitable man John Powers.
>
> Now what has Jane Addams done? Nothing. [Mr. Powers] has been subject to newspaper notoriety by you Jane Addams who has long since forgot the pride and dignity so much admired in a woman.
>
> A Voter

Powers won the 1898 election, but this time he knew he had been in a fight. Jane Addams, who had helped begin the process of reforming Chicago politics, was hailed by millions of fair-minded people for her valiant battle against corruption.

Johnny Powers was wrong about Hull House going out of business within a year. It must be remembered that a century ago there were few government programs to assist needy families. The food, child care, and educational programs Hull House provided were a godsend to thousands of people. Although it was not America's first settlement (New York's Neighborhood Guild, which opened in 1887, had that honor), Hull House was the best-known of these neighborhood outposts. Thanks largely to Hull House's success, the number of settlements in the

Jane Addams was so popular that a brand of canned foods was named for her.

CEDARVILLE AREA
HISTORICAL SOCIETY

United States rose from six in 1892 to well over one hundred in 1900 and to approximately four hundred by 1910.

As Hull House gained fame, so did its director. The public was eager to know more about Jane Addams and her work, so she began writing, eventually producing eleven books and more than five hundred articles. Journalists also wrote about her, competing with one another to heap praise on her.

Famed journalist Ida Tarbell called Miss Addams "the First Lady of the Land." Writers dubbed her "Saint Jane," the "Angel of Democracy," the "Angel of Hull House," and the "Lady of God." Some Hull House neighbors called her "Miss Kind Heart." Early in the twentieth century she was so famous that many American families named their daughters Jane after her.

In the early 1900s, it was a popular pastime for magazines and newspapers to make "most famous people" lists. It was the rare list that didn't include Jane Addams, who was widely considered to be the country's most prominent woman. The March 1908 *Ladies' Home Journal* named her the "First American Woman," ahead of such notables as Helen Keller and Julia Ward Howe, the abolitionist poet who wrote "The Battle Hymn of the Republic" and helped establish Mother's Day in the United States.

Because of her compassion for people, J.A. was often compared to her childhood hero, Abraham Lincoln. There was even talk of running her for president. A 1909 *New York Evening Post* editorial declared: "No one could be a better candidate. As a representative of all the people, she would be ideal. She sympathizes with the rich and poor, with the fortunate and unfortunate."

The Lake Street elevated train stopped at Halsted Street, roughly a mile north of Hull House. It looped around Chicago's business district, carrying tens of thousands of riders every day.
LIBRARY OF CONGRESS

At the end of 1910, the *Chicago Record-Herald* ran an editorial asking "Who are the first five citizens of Chicago?" The newspaper responded: "Of course there can be no doubt of the first—Jane Addams leads all the rest."

No American was more famous for helping others than

Jane Addams, yet much of what she did wasn't generally known during her own lifetime. Her friend Louise deKoven Bowen later said that J.A. did "numberless kind things" with no fanfare. In one example from Hull House's early days, J.A. and Julia Lathrop were called upon to do something out of the ordinary.

The incident began when a young woman ran into Hull House screaming that a friend in the tenement where she lived was about to have a baby. A doctor couldn't be called because the expectant mother—who was just a teenaged girl herself—couldn't pay the bill. Because the young woman was unmarried, her neighbors in the tenement building wouldn't help her, either. The girl's friend begged: Would someone from Hull House come and assist with the birth?

Jane Addams and Julia Lathrop knew little about delivering babies, but they hurried to the tenement to do what they could. Soon they had brought a new person into the world. The young mother was so grateful that she named her baby for the two Hull House women, but since the child was a boy, the name became Julius John instead of Julia Jane.

Jane and Julia felt "stirred by the mystery of birth" as they walked back to Hull House, Jane Addams later wrote. However, J.A. felt a bit shaken. "Doing things that we don't know how to do is going too far," she said to Julia. "Why did we let ourselves be rushed into midwifery?"

"To refuse to respond to a poor girl in the throes of childbirth would be a disgrace to us forevermore," Julia pointed out. "If Hull House does not have its roots in human kindness, it is no good at all."

Everyone knew that children had a special place in J.A.'s heart. Over the years she took a personal interest in hundreds, if not thousands, of neighborhood children: steering them away from trouble, assisting them with their education, and helping them get jobs. Several of the children she aided, including a girl named Hilda Satt Polacheck, later wrote books relating their experiences with Jane Addams and Hull House.

To escape the massacres of Jewish people in Poland, ten-year-old Hilda and her family moved to America in 1892 and settled in an apartment just four blocks from Hull House. Hilda's father soon died, leaving her mother to raise a large family in an area where, according to Hilda, "There was not a tree or a blade of grass anywhere in the neighborhood."

In December 1895, when Hilda was thirteen, an Irish Catholic friend of hers invited her to a Hull House Christmas party. "I might get killed!" protested Hilda, recalling attacks on Jewish people at Christmastime back in Poland.

"I go to Hull House Christmas parties every year, and no one was ever killed," her friend said. Hilda accompanied her friend to the party and enjoyed herself immensely. More than half a century later, in her book *I Came a Stranger: The Story of a Hull-House Girl,* Hilda recalled meeting J.A. at the festivities:

> Then Jane Addams came into the room! It
> was the first time that I looked into those kind,
> understanding eyes. There was a gleam of
> welcome in them that made me feel I was wanted.
> She told us that she was glad we had come. Her

voice was warm and I knew she meant what she
said. We were all poor. Some of us were underfed.
Some of us had holes in our shoes. But we were
not afraid of each other. What greater service can
a human being give than to banish fear from the
heart of a child? Jane Addams did that for me at
that party.

From that moment, Hilda became what she called "a
Hull-House girl" and the settlement became her "oasis in the
desert." She took every class she could, ranging from danc-
ing to Shakespeare, and spent so much time at Hull House
that she practically lived there. Miss Addams even helped
arrange for Hilda to attend the University of Chicago,
and lent her money so that she could quit her job at a shirt
factory. Later, Hilda taught English to immigrants at Hull
House and worked at a Chicago publishing house. Looking
back at how Jane Addams and Hull House had shaped her
life, she wrote:

No one will ever know how many young people
were helped by her wise counsel, how many were
kept out of jail, how many were started on careers
in the arts, in music, in industry, in science, and
above all in [having instilled] in their hearts a true
love of country—a love of service.

Perhaps a letter J.A. saved for forty years best illustrates
how people in trouble turned to Miss Kind Heart. In the spring

of 1895, a young Chicagoan who was in jail wrote to the one
person he believed would come to his aid:

> Chicago
> May 5/95
>
> My dear friend Miss adams I [am] writing these
> few lines to let you know that I am over at the
> County Jail and I am suffering on Bread and
> Water. And if you would be so kind as to send me
> over Tomorow a Basket with some thing to eat i
> will pay you what it cost when i get out and if
> you coud get a lawler to come down to the Case
> Wensday. . . . You are the only friend i got in
> Chicago. And for god sake send me some thing to
> Eat Tomere i am in Cell 38 County Jail Boys
> department.
>
> Saml. Soleycocks

We can't be sure of the outcome, but she wouldn't have been
Jane Addams if she had ignored a plea from a youth who felt
he could count on her.

10

"Let Me Hold Your Foot"

Whenever the Hull House staff wanted to tease Jane Addams about her saintly reputation, someone would say to her, "Let me hold your foot!" This expression, which never failed to annoy her, originated when a woman visiting Hull House was overheard asking, "If you won't let me hold your hand, do let me hold your foot." Apparently, the visitor believed that just by touching the Hull House director, she could obtain some of her saintliness.

The truth was, no one could be as perfect as Jane Addams was reputed to be. Her friends knew that she was a person with problems, peculiarities, and everything else that goes with being human. In fact, the real Jane Addams was in some ways more remarkable and certainly more interesting than the "Saint Jane" portrayed in newspapers and magazines.

Physically, J.A. had changed a great deal from the days when she weighed a frail ninety-eight pounds. By 1895, thirty-five-year-old Jane Addams had grown plump. Her doctors warned that she was getting too heavy, but whether she was at a fund-raising dinner or having supper in the Hull House Residents'

Dining Hall, Miss Addams loved to eat. She kept a chart of her weight in an effort to control it, but the numbers continued to go in the wrong direction until she eventually topped two hundred pounds.

Addams still experienced periods of depression long after Hull House opened, but she found a way to deal with her bad moods. She would rearrange the pictures and furniture in the various Hull House buildings, which always took her mind off her troubles. Twice while rearranging things, she toppled off a tall stepladder, once breaking her arm, yet she always went back to redecorating as a way to relax.

While the public saw her gentle side, Jane Addams could be plenty tough—especially if Hull House's welfare was at stake. Since the settlement house depended on donations for its continued existence, she was constantly appealing to her rich friends for contributions—often pestering them until they wrote checks just to get her off their backs. She had a long memory, reminding people of their past promises, as this letter to Chicagoan Nettie Fowler McCormick illustrates:

> Hull-House
> 335 South Halsted Street
> Chicago
>
> My dear Mrs. McCormick,
>   Last March you very kindly promised to give fifty dollars a year, for three years to Hull-House toward its general expenses. You have given us some money since then for new things, so that it

seems almost ungrateful to collect this. But the time is here, and we would be very glad indeed to have the check. . . .

> I am very sincerely yours,
> Jane Addams

The note served its purpose. Less than a week later, J.A. scribbled at the bottom of her copy of the letter: "Sent check for $50."

J.A. could be even pushier than that! After convincing William Kent to tear down his tenement buildings and to allow his land to be made into a children's playground, J.A. had another request: Would he continue to pay the taxes on the property? Kent was astonished. Hadn't he done enough already? How could she expect him to pay the taxes on land that was no longer his? No doubt she told him her philosophy: It was the duty of the rich to help the less fortunate. Whatever she said worked, for Kent agreed to pay the property taxes.

Despite their friendship, J.A. and Helen Culver had a stormy relationship at times. Like William Kent, Miss Culver thought she had been extremely generous. Hadn't she given the Hull mansion and the land on which it stood to Jane Addams, as well as other lots she owned in the neighborhood? Yet J.A. was never satisfied, and kept asking her to pay for repairs on the house and contribute money to the settlement. On one occasion a fed-up Miss Culver sent J.A. an angry letter:

> My Dear Miss Addams:—
> I regret that my benevolent purposes—

represented by gifts amounting to about
$350.00—have been productive only of
disappointment—and judging from your note,
of an impression among your acquaintances
that I entertain toward your enterprise the
relation of delinquent landlady.

Yours Very Truly,
Helen Culver

J.A. immediately wrote an apologetic letter to Miss Culver. "Asking for money is new to me and I am afraid I do not do it well," she explained, adding that "I hope you will not consider me ungrateful." The apology worked, for Miss Culver soon sent another note saying that "if it will add to the comfort and pleasure of your occupancy," J.A. could have the sum of money she requested.

Jane Addams practiced what she preached. During her forty-six years as director of Hull House, she refused to accept even a penny in salary for herself. She also donated most of her personal funds to the settlement. She had a roof over her head, clothes, food, and some of her inheritance left, so why have a large bank account when the money could help the poor?

Money wasn't all that J.A. gave away. She was a compulsive giver. For example, she received many Christmas gifts, but according to Louise deKoven Bowen, she "always gave away everything, almost before she thanked the person for it." She even gave away her own clothes. Although not the most fashionable dresser, J.A. did like to wear elbow-length white

Jane Addams, circa 1896.

SWARTHMORE COLLEGE PEACE COLLECTION, JANE ADDAMS COLLECTION

gloves, which made her feel a little stylish. Knowing that J.A. was fond of white gloves but was always misplacing them, Mrs. Bowen presented her with a dozen pairs as a gift.

Several days later J.A. asked Mrs. Bowen to lend her a pair of white gloves. "But I just gave you a dozen pair!" said her friend. She had given them all away, Jane Addams explained.

Mrs. Bowen thought of something that Jane would *have* to keep. She had overheard J.A. say that she needed to shop for underwear. Mrs. Bowen later recalled:

> That was at a time when women wore considerably more than they do at present, and I had a dozen of almost everything worn by women made up to fit Miss Addams and marked "JA" so that she could not give it away. On Christmas Day she asked a number of the residents to her room and was handing out all these carefully made pieces [of underwear] when I bounded in. I did persuade her to keep a few in order that she might have something to wear herself.

J.A. often raised money by going on speaking tours, which sometimes lasted weeks. She lectured in dozens of cities in the United States and England. Her fee around the year 1900 was $25 per talk (which would equal about $500 in today's money) plus traveling expenses.

Audiences enjoyed J.A.'s relaxed speaking style. Even when addressing a packed auditorium, she spoke as though she were

out that the laws of the United States extended to all citizens, no matter how unpopular their views. She helped Mr. Isaak obtain a lawyer and win his freedom, for he had had nothing to do with the president's murder.

J.A.'s courage was again demonstrated in the summer of 1919, when Chicago suffered a terrible race riot. For several days white and black mobs terrorized Chicago neighborhoods, setting fires and beating and killing people. Twenty-three black people and fifteen whites were killed, hundreds of Chicagoans were severely injured, and a thousand homes were burned.

Few black people lived in the Hull House neighborhood at the time of the riot. However, a gang of white thugs burst into the settlement, intending to beat up or maybe kill a black man who worked as a cook in the Hull House kitchen.

At the original Hull House, which today is a museum, the manager spoke to us with pride about how Jane Addams rescued this man from the gang. "She hid the cook under her bed," explained Dan Portincaso. The thugs went from room to room searching for the cook. When they reached Miss Addams's bedroom, she blocked the doorway and refused to let the troublemakers inside.

"Gentlemen, I'm a lady. I would never hide a man in my bedroom," she said. Satisfied that the cook was not there, the ruffians left the house. The cook was then taken out a side door and driven to his home by a husband and wife who were both Hull House residents.

Jane Addams did more than save a man from a mob in those violent days of July 1919. "She marched down the street during the riot speaking to people and trying to calm them," con-

Ida B. Wells-Barnett.
DONALD DUSTER

tinued Dan Portincaso. While J.A. spoke to the white rioters, an African American friend of hers, civil rights leader Ida B. Wells-Barnett, roamed the black neighborhoods calming people. After about a week, the riot finally ended.

Dan also mentioned a little-known fact about J.A. and her stepmother. "Anna never came to Hull House," he said. "Not once." Besides blaming Jane for her younger son's mental illness, Anna disapproved of her stepdaughter's work at the settlement. Anna believed in class distinctions and thought it was wrong for a woman from a wealthy family to mix with the poor.

For her part, Jane tried to maintain a good relationship with her stepmother. She visited Anna during her periodic trips to Cedarville and sent her letters. For example, on March 15, 1910, she wrote to "My dear Mother" saying that "I am planning to come to Cedarville next Monday—March 21st—to stay until Wednesday. . . . With much love to yourself, I am always your loving daughter, Jane Addams."

In fact, the thousands of letters in the Jane Addams Papers reveal that J.A. remained closely involved with all her relatives. Every few days she wrote to her sister Alice Addams Haldeman. She also oversaw financial affairs for the family of her deceased sister Mary Addams Linn. She took her nephew Stanley Linn with her on some of her speaking tours and often went to care for relatives in times of illness. On December 26, 1911, she took a young grandnephew to Chicago's Michael Reese Hospital to have his tonsils removed. While waiting for the surgery to be completed, J.A. obtained some hospital stationery and wrote three letters, one to her niece Marcet Haldeman and two others to friends.

If J.A. was someone's friend, she was a friend for life. She kept in touch with dozens of people—classmates from Rockford Female Seminary, friends she made through her work at Hull House, and men and women she encountered on her speaking tours and travels. By 1912, one of J.A.'s oldest friends, Flora Guiteau, had fallen on hard times. Jane sent her a check for $100 (equal to about $2,000 in today's money) so that Flora could pay her bills. Flora, whose half brother had assassinated President James Garfield thirty-one years earlier, wrote to Jane explaining that the money was "such a comfort," adding that "I'm so proud of what you have done."

J.A.'s closest friend was Mary Rozet Smith. The two of them often traveled together, and J.A. was a regular guest at the home of Mary's parents on Walton Place in Chicago. "The Smiths more or less adopted Jane Addams," Dan Portincaso explained. When apart, Jane and Mary wrote each other long letters. In March 1910 alone, six of the fourteen letters J.A. wrote were to Mary.

That J.A. and Mary Rozet Smith were each other's best friends was common knowledge. Some people believe they

Mary Rozet Smith with her niece.

SWARTHMORE COLLEGE PEACE COLLECTION, JANE ADDAMS COLLECTION

were also lovers—that they were what today we would call a lesbian couple. There are sharp disagreements among those who claim J.A. was gay, those who say she was not, and those who insist that we just don't know.

Those who believe J.A. was a lesbian point out that she destroyed much of her correspondence with Mary, presumably because it revealed intimate details of their relationship. As it is, the surviving letters contain numerous references that can be interpreted as romantic. J.A. addressed Mary as "Darling" and "Dearest" when writing to her. And in a letter that J.A. did not destroy, Mary Rozet Smith confessed to her in December 1896:

> Dearest Lady
>
> I came home [from being with J.A.] with quite a glow at my heart. You can never know what it is to me to have had you and to have you now. I only hope I am thankful enough. I'm given to turning sentimental at this season, as you know, and I feel quite a rush of emotion when I think of you. I have been having another bad time with my conscience about my "wealth" and I've been in the depths of gloom until yesterday when the sight and sound of you cured me. I seem to be slipping into melancholy, but I'm really hilariously cheerful and full of gratitude to you and overflowing with affection.
>
> Yours always,
> Mary R.S.

Those who believe J.A. and Mary were lovers point out that they shared a summer home in Bar Harbor, Maine. In addition, J.A. was never known to show any romantic interest in a man. With all these "clues," some authors have concluded that the two women had a romantic relationship. In his book about Chicago, *City of the Century,* Donald L. Miller simply asserts, "Lifelong friends, Addams and Smith were quite likely lovers as well."

Others point out that a century or more ago it was common for women to have very close friendships with other women, and to openly express their affection for one another even when it was not romantic love. J.A. destroyed much of her correspondence with Miss Smith for reasons we will never know, they say, and we shouldn't read too much into a few affectionate words like "Darling" and "Dearest." In her book *Jane Addams and the Dream of American Democracy,* Jean Bethke Elshtain states: "Celibate lives need not be lonely lives but could be full of love, friendship, and joy—and so they were for Jane Addams, for Ellen Gates Starr, for Addams's companion, Mary Rozet Smith, and for many other educated women of their day."

There is another mystery about J.A.: What was her religion? She attended Methodist services as a child, was later baptized into the Cedarville Presbyterian Church, yet told some people she was a Quaker. And whenever anyone suggested that she hold religious services at Hull House, J.A. would reply: "What kind of service? Episcopal—Presbyterian—Catholic—Congregational—or what?"

Her friend Louise deKoven Bowen explained that J.A.

attended various churches, going to this one on one Sunday, another the following week, and perhaps yet another the week after that. "She believed in God and talked a great deal about Him," explained Mrs. Bowen. "But she felt the best way to practice her religion was to live it."

11

"Because of What You Are and Stand For"

By the early 1900s, J.A. was venturing into other activities besides running Hull House.

When in her twenties, she had written a number of articles, but no magazine would accept them. Now that she headed Hull House, she had something to write about, and magazines, newspapers, and book publishers clamored for her work. Besides her experiences at Hull House, J.A. wrote about such subjects as child labor, poverty, women's suffrage (the right to vote), and world peace.

Between the 1890s and 1935, J.A. published approximately five hundred articles—an average of more than ten per year. Over a thirty-three-year period, she published eleven books— one every three years. Her first book, *Democracy and Social Ethics* (1902), expressed her view that people in a democracy are like a huge extended family. Her favorite of all her books, *The Spirit of Youth and the City Streets* (1909), praised the

Hull House Library.

SWARTHMORE COLLEGE PEACE COLLECTION, JANE ADDAMS COLLECTION

energy and enthusiasm of young people while condemning urban conditions that deprived them of a good education and safe places to play. J.A.'s famous autobiography *Twenty Years at Hull-House* was published in 1910. She produced all this despite being, in her own words, a "bungling writer" who worked "so slowly and painfully."

J.A. had unusual writing methods. Often she began by discussing a topic in a speech. After she had delivered the talk dozens of times, gradually improving it, she might write it out as an article. Her sister Alice's daughter, Marcet Haldeman, reported that the woman she addressed as "Dearest Auntie" assembled her books much the way an artisan pieces together a quilt. First, J.A. would produce a long manuscript in which she discussed various aspects of a topic without worrying about the order. Then she would divide her manuscript into coherent chunks, each of which might be a chapter. She would rearrange them until they were in a pleasing order, adding new transitions so that the whole thing read smoothly.

Because of J.A.'s enormous fame, it might be assumed that her books sold millions of copies. The royalty statements she saved reveal the truth. Generally, her books sold several thousand copies. In a typical year she earned perhaps a thousand dollars from her books, and a few hundred dollars from her articles.

Meanwhile, in the early twentieth century the United States was the scene of three powerful social movements: the battle for equal rights for African Americans, the struggle for women's right to vote, and the campaign for world peace. Jane Addams took part in all three movements.

Addams thought it shameful that African Americans were treated as second-class citizens. She was a co-founder of the National Association for the Advancement of Colored People (NAACP), an organization begun in 1909 to fight for the rights of black people. J.A. also arranged for black leaders to speak at Hull House. She didn't bring in those conservative black spokesmen who were popular with whites because they advised their people to be patient about gaining their rights. She brought in militant black leaders, including author and educator W.E.B. Du Bois and anti-lynching crusader Ida B. Wells-Barnett, both of whom believed that blacks should

Scholar and author W.E.B. Du Bois and anti-lynching crusader Ida B. Wells-Barnett were, like Jane Addams, co-founders of the National Association for the Advancement of Colored People.

LIBRARY OF CONGRESS

demand equality. Like Mrs. Wells-Barnett, Jane Addams spoke out against lynching—the murder of a person by a mob, usually for racial reasons.

J.A. also entered the battle for women's right to vote. She

became friends with prominent suffragists, including Susan B. Anthony and Carrie Chapman Catt. In 1911, J.A. became vice president of the National American Woman Suffrage Association, and in that capacity she traveled through Illinois, Wisconsin, and other states speaking on women's voting rights. She took up her pen for the cause, too. One of her best articles, "If Men Were Seeking the Franchise" (another term for suffrage), appeared in the June 1913 *Ladies' Home Journal*. It turned the tables by pretending what it would be like if men, not women, were deprived of the vote. To men who wanted to vote, J.A. pointed out:

> You are so fond of fighting—you always have been since you were little boys. [If you were allowed to vote] you'd very likely forget that the real object of the State is to nurture and protect life, and you would be voting away huge sums of money for battleships, each costing ten million dollars, more money than all the buildings of Harvard University. Every time a gun is fired in a battleship, it expends, or rather explodes, seventeen hundred dollars, as much as a college education costs, and yet you would be firing off these guns as mere salutes, with no enemy within three thousand miles, simply because you so enjoy the sound of shooting.

Jane even appeared in a movie about suffrage. Released in 1912, this silent film dramatized how granting women the right to vote would eliminate sweatshops and improve life for poor families.

Back in the 1890s, J.A. had entered the political arena by opposing Nineteenth Ward boss Johnny Powers. Early in the twentieth century, she turned her attention to national politics. Like her father before her, she generally supported the Republicans, the party of Abraham Lincoln. In the early 1900s, J.A. became friends with one of the leading Republicans of the time, Theodore Roosevelt.

Roosevelt, who served as the nation's vice president in 1901 and as its twenty-sixth president from 1901 to 1909, visited Hull House several times. He toured the Hull House kindergarten, met with a large number of Boy Scouts, and listened to the fifty-member Hull House Boys' Club Band. He also enjoyed theatrical performances by the Hull House Players.

In 1912, J.A. appeared before the platform committee of the Republican National Convention, which was held in Chicago that summer. She tried but failed to convince the Republicans to insert a women's suffrage plank into their platform. At the same time, Theodore Roosevelt was also disappointed in the Republican Party for a number of reasons. He decided to seek the nation's highest office under the banner of a new political party. Officially called the Progressive Party, it was nicknamed the Bull Moose Party because of Roosevelt's boast that he felt "as strong as a bull moose."

The former president ran on a platform calling for women's suffrage, the outlawing of child labor, an eight-hour workday for men and women, the improvement of housing, and other measures that he said would benefit the "public welfare."

Jane Addams (right) led an eight-woman delegation to the Republican National Convention in 1912.

CHICAGO HISTORICAL MUSEUM, DAILY NEWS COLLECTION

These were "all things I have been fighting for for more than a decade," J.A. told the *New York Post*. She decided to support Roosevelt in his long-shot campaign against the candidates of the two main parties: President William Howard Taft, whom the Republicans nominated for a second term, and Democratic challenger Woodrow Wilson.

J.A. joined the Roosevelt campaign, and at the Progressive

Party Convention, held at the Chicago Coliseum on August 5–7, 1912, she seconded Roosevelt's nomination. This marked the first time a woman had ever seconded a nomination for a major presidential candidate. In her seconding speech, J.A. declared that she supported Theodore Roosevelt's candidacy because

> A great party has pledged itself to the protection of children, to the care of the aged, to the relief of overworked girls, to the safeguarding of burdened men. Committed to these humane undertakings, it is inevitable that such a party should appeal to women, should seek to draw upon their moral energy.

The day after the convention ended, Theodore Roosevelt sent J.A. a telegram. "I wish to thank you for seconding me," he wrote. "I prized your action not only because of what you are and stand for, but because of what it symbolizes for the new movement."

Prior to the election, J.A. wrote many newspaper and magazine articles explaining why she supported Theodore Roosevelt and the new Progressive Party. Her support meant so much to the campaign that groups of women who performed at Progressive Party rallies called themselves "Jane Addams Choruses" and sang from what was known as the "Jane Addams Song Book." One of the most popular songs performed by the Jane Addams Choruses bore the name of the Progressive Party's presidential candidate:

Roosevelt
(to the tune of "O Tannenbaum")

Thou wilt not cower in the dust,
Roosevelt, O Roosevelt;
Thy gleaming sword shall never rust,
Roosevelt, O Roosevelt;
In thee we hail a leader just,
In thee repose a sacred trust,
To crush the powers of greed and lust,
Roosevelt, O Roosevelt!

But Addams's greatest contribution to Theodore Roosevelt's campaign was speechmaking. Between October 3 and November 4 she was in almost constant motion. Traveling by train, she urged voters in thirty cities in fifteen states to elect the Progressive ticket.

On Election Day—November 5, 1912—Theodore Roosevelt went down to defeat. The popular vote totals showed Woodrow Wilson in first place with 6.3 million, Roosevelt second with 4.2 million, and William Howard Taft last with 3.5 million. In the electoral college, where the nation's presidential elections are ultimately decided, Wilson won the nation's highest office with 435 votes, while Roosevelt tallied 88 and Taft had just 8.

J.A. was not terribly disappointed by the result. Theodore Roosevelt had made an excellent showing for a third-party candidate. Besides, the campaign had won many converts to the causes of women's suffrage, children's rights, and other issues dear to Jane Addams's heart.

Presidential candidate Theodore Roosevelt at Chicago's Union Station in 1912.
LIBRARY OF CONGRESS

Millions of Americans were angry and disturbed over Addams's role in the election, however. Republicans resented her for taking part in a campaign that siphoned off many Republican votes, perhaps costing Taft the election. People who had called her "Saint Jane" were disappointed that she had stepped off her pedestal to participate in the "dirty" world of politics. And of course there were many people who still considered politics a male domain where a woman simply didn't belong.

Over the next few years, Jane Addams would devote herself to another cause that would stir up far more anger against her.

12

"The Cause of Peace"

One summer, the staff kept count and discovered that a thousand tourists a day came to see Hull House and to glimpse Jane Addams.

Louise deKoven Bowen told a story about a group of visitors who were led into Hull House by a tour guide who wasn't very knowledgeable. After telling the tourists a little about the settlement, the guide explained that its founder, Jane Addams, *had been* a wonderful woman.

"How long has Miss Addams been dead?" asked a startled sightseer.

"Oh, three or four years," answered the guide.

Overhearing the conversation, J.A. came from an adjacent room and appeared before the group of tourists. "I am sorry to disappoint you," she said good-naturedly, "but I assure you I am very much alive!"

Although definitely "very much alive," Addams wasn't devoting nearly as much time to Hull House as she had in earlier days. Each year, she still wrote hundreds of fund-raising letters on behalf of the settlement house. She also oversaw the frequent repairs required by the complex's thirteen buildings, attended many Hull House club meetings, plays, and concerts, and always tried to be there for the Christmas and other holiday programs. As the years passed, however, she trusted her staff to manage much of the day-to-day Hull House business, which freed her to pursue other interests.

In about 1904, Mary Rozet Smith had purchased a house for herself and Jane Addams in Bar Harbor, Maine. Each summer the two women left the city behind and went to their vacation home, where J.A. worked on her books and articles and caught up on her letter writing. At other times of the year, she visited her nieces and nephews or went on speaking tours to campaign for women's suffrage. When she reached her mid-fifties, she took up a new cause that became as important to her as her work with Hull House: the peace movement. In fact, over the last twenty years of her life, J.A. probably devoted as much time and energy to the quest for peace as she did to Hull House.

During the early 1900s, a number of nations engaged in military buildups and clashes over disputed territory. In July 1914, war broke out and quickly escalated. On one side was a group of countries designated the Central Powers, which included Austria-Hungary, Germany, Bulgaria, and the Ottoman Empire (what is now Turkey). Against them were the Allies, which included Great Britain, France, Belgium, Russia, and eventually twenty other countries.

Called the Great War by those who lived through it and who hoped it was the war to end all wars, it is now referred to as World War I. The conflict turned into the bloodiest war ever

A peace parade in New York City in the early 1900s.
LIBRARY OF CONGRESS

fought up to that time. New weapons such as battleships, machine guns, flamethrowers, poison gas, submarines, fighter airplanes, and tanks claimed huge numbers of lives on both sides. On average, about six thousand soldiers were killed and nearly fifteen thousand were wounded *each day* that the war continued. The death count among civilians was also incredibly high—equal to the number of military fatalities, according to some estimates.

People in the United States were divided over the war. Many Americans wanted their country to side with its traditional friends, England and France, against Germany and the other Central Powers. Many others felt that the war didn't concern them and that the United States should remain neutral.

Like most Americans, Jane Addams was shocked by the bloodshed. What made the war especially disturbing to her was that Hull House operated on the principles of brotherhood and cooperation among people of diverse backgrounds. If human beings of various ethnic groups could get along at Hull House, why couldn't they do so on the world stage?

Everyone knew that Jane Addams would condemn the war and oppose U.S. involvement in it. Seven years earlier, in 1907, she had expressed her pacifist beliefs in her book *Newer Ideals of Peace*. The question was: What would Jane Addams *do* to oppose the war?

She began by helping to organize a group of Chicagoans into a peace committee. On December 14, 1914, Jane Addams wrote a letter to famed suffragist Carrie Chapman Catt in which she declared that she was dedicated to "the cause of peace." Addams added: "The Emergency Peace Committee which we have organized in Chicago is doing very well. I hope that very shortly we may issue some sort of a call."

At the end of 1914, Miss Addams and Mrs. Catt sent a "call" to women's groups around the country. Their letter invited women to gather early the following year in Washington, D.C., "to consider organizing a National Peace Committee of Women." This was to be a females-only meeting, for J.A. believed that what she called their "nurturing instinct" made women especially fit to lead the peace movement. Mrs. Catt agreed and confided to Miss Addams that it was "an excellent idea to have the [peace meeting] conducted by women alone."

J.A. traveled by train to Washington, D.C., where the peace conference was held on January 10, 1915, in the ballroom of the Willard Hotel. Three thousand women from across the United States attended the conference. They formed an organization called the Woman's Peace Party and elected Jane Addams as its president. In a speech to the huge audience, she said:

> From the time a soldier is born to the moment he marches in his uniform to be destroyed, it is largely the women of his household who have cared for him. War not only overthrows the work of the mother, the nurse, and the teacher, but at the same time ruthlessly destroys the very conception of the nurture of life. . . .
>
> Many of us believe that throughout this world of ours thousands of men and women have become convinced that the sacrifice of life in wartime is unnecessary. It is possible that if women in Europe—in the very countries which are now at war—receive a message from the women of America solemnly protesting against this sacrifice, they may take courage to formulate their own [protests].

Before the day ended, the women did "formulate a statement of their convictions"—embodied in what they called their Peace Platform. Its preamble declared:

> We, women of the United States, assembled in
> behalf of World Peace, grateful for the security
> of our own country, but sorrowing for the misery
> of all involved in the present struggle among
> warring nations, do hereby band ourselves
> together to demand that war be abolished. As
> women, we are particularly charged with the
> future of childhood and with the care of the
> helpless and the unfortunate. We will no longer
> endure without protest that added burden of
> maimed and invalid men and poverty-stricken
> widows and orphans which [war creates].

The Peace Platform offered several specific suggestions. One was that the neutral countries hold a convention as soon as possible for the purpose of finding a way to guide the warring nations toward peace. The Woman's Peace Party also advocated what it called "continuous mediation"—nonstop talks until the war ended.

A few weeks after the creation of the Woman's Peace Party in Washington, D.C., Jane Addams received a cablegram from Dr. Aletta Jacobs, who was one of the first female physicians in the Netherlands as well as a peace activist. In late April and early May of 1915, an international peace meeting was to be held at The Hague, a city in the Netherlands that was a popular site for conferences. As the president of the largest women's peace organization in the United States, Jane Addams was invited to head the meeting at The Hague and bring a delegation of women with her.

The spring of 1915 was a difficult time for Jane Addams. Over the previous few years, illness and death had continued to claim family members. George Haldeman, her stepbrother and inseparable childhood companion, had died in late 1909 at the age of only forty-eight. Jane's brother Weber still suffered from what court documents called "undue mental excitement." Institutionalized for many years, he would die at an Illinois state hospital for the insane in 1918. After a long struggle with cancer, Jane's sister Alice Addams Haldeman lay near death in early 1915. J.A. went to Girard, Kansas, to be with her lone remaining sister during her last days. Alice died in March. Following the funeral, which was held in Cedarville, Jane Addams returned to Chicago. Still grieving for her sister, she did her best to prepare for the Netherlands trip, which was just three weeks away.

Addams sent some last-minute letters to women she hoped would accompany her. Writing to New York settlement worker Lillian Wald, J.A. revealed her fears about the upcoming conference and echoed her motto from her college days nearly forty years earlier: Always do what you are afraid to do.

March 26, 1915

Dear Lady:—

I am awfully sorry that you have decided not to go to The Hague. The undertaking, of course, offers many possibilities of failure. I think that women who are willing to fail may be able to break through that curious hypnotic spell which

makes it impossible for any of the nations to consider Peace. It would be a great thing for us if you
would go with us!

J.A. had better luck convincing other women to go overseas.
Two Hull House residents agreed to accompany her to The
Hague: Dr. Alice Hamilton, who was a physician, and Grace
Abbott, who headed an organization called the Immigrants'
Protective League. All told, forty-six prominent American
women, including professors, lawyers, authors and editors,
and social workers, agreed to go to The Hague with Addams.

The American women sailed from New York City aboard a
Dutch steamship, the SS *Noordam,* on April 16, 1915. J.A.
passed the time by planning her speeches and writing letters to
Marcet Haldeman, the only child of her deceased sister Alice.
For the rest of her life, J.A. would correspond with her niece
Marcet, much as she had done with Marcet's mother.

The *Noordam* crossed the ocean without incident but
encountered trouble when approaching the Netherlands. A
British gunboat came alongside and, aiming a machine gun at
her, forbade the *Noordam* to land. J.A. protested vehemently,
but not until the British were convinced that no German spies
were aboard did they allow the *Noordam* to continue on to the
Netherlands.

Approximately fifteen hundred women from twelve different
countries attended the peace conference, which opened at The
Hague on April 28, 1915. The delegates included women from
neutral nations such as the United States, and also from the
warring countries such as Germany, Great Britain, Belgium,

Jane Addams (front row, second from left) and other delegates to the First International Congress of Women at The Hague in 1915.

SWARTHMORE COLLEGE PEACE COLLECTION, JANE ADDAMS COLLECTION

and Austria. The conference marked the start of the Women's International League for Peace and Freedom (WILPF). The delegates passed several resolutions, including a "protest against the madness and the horror of war" and a recommendation that "continuous mediation" begin immediately.

Jane Addams, who was chosen to head the new organization, made a stirring presidential address. All the women at the conference were praiseworthy, J.A. began, but what made this event an especially "high and precious moment in human experience" was the fact that women from warring nations had gathered together. This was a brave act, because people who met with the enemy in wartime risked being called unpatriotic or even traitors.

The women at the conference had a crucial mission, Miss Addams pointed out, for the war jeopardized the future of "the human race as a whole." Thanks to newspapers, photographs, and motion pictures, she continued, "Never before has the world known so fearfully and so minutely what war means to the soldier, to women and children, to civilization." The problem was, while most people wanted to end the bloodshed, the war had taken on a life of its own, and governments seemed helpless to act. Who would stop the madness if not the women of the world? And if the women didn't act, she concluded:

> The time may come when the survivors of the
> war may well reproach women for their inaction
> during this terrible time. It is possible they will
> then say that when devotion to the ideals of
> patriotism drove thousands of men into
> international warfare, the women refused to
> accept the challenge and in that moment failed
> to assert courageously the sanctity of human life.

Before the meeting ended on May 1, the women began to carry out their plan of "continuous mediation." They formed two important committees. One was sent out to speak to government leaders of countries that were still neutral, to urge them to remain so. The other, which was headed by Jane Addams and Dr. Aletta Jacobs, was dispatched to meet with leaders of the warring nations.

Accompanied by several colleagues, Addams and Jacobs embarked on one of the most unusual wartime missions ever. For about two months they visited countries on both sides of the conflict. As they crisscrossed borders, they saw firsthand

An early logo for the Women's International League for Peace and Freedom.

WOMEN'S INTERNATIONAL LEAGUE FOR PEACE AND FREEDOM, UNITED STATES

the terrible results of the fighting: hungry children, bombed cities, wounded people, and families missing fathers, sons, and brothers. They visited several European capitals on their journey. In London they met with the British prime minister. In Berlin they spoke with the imperial chancellor of Germany. Other stops included Vienna, Budapest, Rome, and Paris.

Except for the French foreign minister, the European leaders seemed "ready to stop the war immediately if some honorable method of securing peace were provided," J.A. later told her nephew James Weber Linn. The most receptive leader J.A. and Jacobs met was Prime Minister Karl Count von Stuergkh of Austria, who sat silently pondering their presentation.

Believing that he had rejected their talk of peace, Jane Addams said, "It perhaps seems to you very foolish that women should go about in this way. But after all, the world is so strange in this war that our mission may be no more strange or foolish than the rest."

Suddenly, the Austrian prime minister slammed his fist on the table. "Foolish?" he repeated. "Not at all. These are the first sensible words that have been uttered in this room for ten months. That door opens from time to time and people come in to say, 'Mr. Minister, we must have more men, more ammunition, more money, or we cannot go on with this war.' At last the door opens and two people walk in and say, 'Mr. Minister, why not substitute negotiations for fighting?' *You* are the sensible ones!"

Upon returning home in the summer of 1915, Jane Addams was optimistic that peace might soon be made. The conversations she and Dr. Jacobs had had with European leaders were

JANE ADDAMS

at best just tiny steps toward ending the war, she realized. Her great hope was that President Woodrow Wilson would take the lead in convincing the warring nations to talk. J.A. corresponded with President Wilson and even met with him in Washington, D.C. Although disappointed that he would not yet act as peacemaker, she was grateful that he seemed determined to keep the United States out of the conflict. But that wouldn't be easy. In May 1915, while J.A. had been in Europe on her peace mission, a German submarine had sunk the British ocean liner *Lusitania,* killing approximately 1,200 passengers, including 128 Americans. President Wilson convinced Germany to stop attacking passenger ships, while maintaining America's neutrality in the war.

As head of both the Woman's Peace Party of the United States and the new international league, J.A. continued her peace efforts over the next two years. She wrote hundreds of letters to gather support for the peace movement, convincing some influential people to donate to the cause. For example, on November 22, 1915, automaker Henry Ford and his wife, Clara, sent a $2,000 check to J.A. "to be used in your peace campaign."

J.A. also organized peace conferences. On January 9–11, 1916, she presided over the first annual Woman's Peace Party convention in Washington, D.C. Their group had more power than they realized, J.A. said in her presidential address. Many movements have started out small, only to grow larger and more powerful until lawmakers were forced to take notice of them.

After the convention ended, Addams remained in the nation's capital. On January 13, she testified before the United States

Upon her return from the Netherlands peace conference,
Jane Addams spoke to reporters at Chicago's Union Station.
LIBRARY OF CONGRESS

House of Representatives Committee on Military Affairs about a proposed bill to strengthen the military in case the country entered the war. "As president of the Woman's Peace Party," she said, she was speaking "for many women in all parts of the country" who wanted the United States to stay out of the conflict.

"Our war contagion is like the case of a man living in Kansas," she told the congressmen, "who, hearing that there were a great many burglaries in New York City, immediately armed himself against burglars, although there were none in Kansas." In other words, why should the United States gear up for a war that was being fought three thousand miles away in Europe? The congressmen listened politely but decided to strengthen the military just in case.

As long as the United States remained out of the war, Jane Addams had the support of a large segment of the population. The following are just two of the many letters J.A. saved praising her peace efforts:

Miami, Florida
December 6, 1915

Miss Jane Addams
Chicago, Ill.

Dear Miss Addams,

This letter is written by one who has felt the horror of war. Through the Spanish-American War I lost an adored husband and a grand, good father, both of whom passed out by the door of anguish unspeakable. One of my sisters also became a widow, her husband being shot on the battlefield leaving a little baby, born during his absence.

For your grand and earnest work I thank you in the name of every maimed and broken man, every fatherless child and every weary and sad-hearted woman brought to this condition by the horrors of war.

Yours truly,
Lucy K. Kellogg

Kaukauna, Wisconsin
March 30, 1917

My Dear Miss Addams,

I have read so much about you and the good you have done in connection with the peace league in our country. As a mother of sons I urge you and all peace workers to do all you can towards keeping this country from war. It seems mothers are perfectly helpless in that matter. We are supposed to hand over our sons whenever war agitators think we need some bloodshed. It seems terrible that our young men the best in the country must be slain, like sheep led to the slaughter, and the world now must have broken hearted mothers by the score, never to be healed.

Oh! I hope and pray our country will keep out of war and not become a military nation. May God forbid! This is from a plain mother, but if my few words would make any impression towards peace, please send [this letter] to the President or Mrs. Wilson.

Sincerely,
from a mother of sons

Just a few days after "a mother of sons" wrote to J.A., the situation changed dramatically. During the winter of 1916–17, President Wilson had stepped up his efforts to end the war, with no success. In fact, the greatest fears of Jane Addams and millions of other Americans came to pass: Germany resumed its submarine attacks on nonmilitary vessels, including American ships, in early 1917. Several U.S. ships were sunk. On April 2, 1917, President Wilson asked Congress to declare war on Germany. The declaration was issued four days later, and America joined the Allies in their war against Germany and the other Central Powers.

It was one thing to oppose the conflict as long as the United States remained neutral, but quite another to oppose it once the nation was at war. The country instituted a draft that eventually called men ages eighteen through forty-five for military service. Out of a total U.S. population of 100 million, more than 4.7 million men and women served in the armed forces during the Great War. There was a widespread feeling that, regardless of what they might have thought before, all Americans owed it to the men and women in service to support the war effort. People who still argued for peace were called "unpatriotic," "German sympathizers," and "slackers."

Everyone wondered whether Jane Addams would change her views and join the vast majority or continue opposing the war despite U.S. involvement. The decision of the nation's most famous woman was important, for it could influence many other people.

It was an easy but life-changing choice. Instead of trying to win the war, she believed, everyone should work to end it. Addams continued to use her voice and pen to promote peace. On April 16, 1917, just ten days after the United States declared war, J.A. and twenty-two other pacifists sent a letter

During the Great War, newspaper cartoons made fun of pacifists.

to President Wilson, complaining that they were being deprived of their freedom of speech by their fellow Americans, including public officials.

"Halls have been refused [to pacifists] for public discussion," the petition pointed out, "meetings have been broken up, speakers have been arrested." It was vital that "the spirit of democracy not be broken," the letter asserted, and that Americans remember that the minority had the right to express their opinions.

Relatively few people were in the mood for J.A.'s peace talk. She was bombarded with criticism for her pacifism. People went so far as to call her a traitor and to threaten her life. A more thoughtful letter complaining about her actions came from an elderly man in Kirkwood, Illinois:

May 11, 1917

Dear Miss Addams,

Being the father of two sons, who will be called on to defend our beloved country, and being myself a veteran of the Civil War, I protest against a person of your prominence intending to embarrass our efforts for national defense. We have been attacked. What would you have us do?

Although there is no record that she responded to him, we know from J.A.'s writings how she might have answered. We must keep the lines of communication open, she might say— with each other and with the enemy—and keep talking about peace until a way is found to achieve it. Otherwise, as the killing continues on both sides, hatreds will deepen and the adversaries will keep fighting, perhaps not even remembering what they are battling *for*.

She was especially hurt by criticism from people who had been her friends. Theodore Roosevelt, whom she had supported in his run for president in 1912, turned against her. He said that she was part of the "shrieking sisterhood" and called her "poor bleeding Jane" because of her pacifist views. Making a nasty joke at J.A.'s expense, the former Bull Moose Party candidate referred to her as a "Bull Mouse."

Louise deKoven Bowen, who had been her friend and chief

Hull House supporter for twenty-five years, grew angry with J.A. for not supporting America in the war. The two women kept their falling-out to themselves, but several years later Mrs. Bowen wrote J.A. a letter mentioning "that horrid time of the war when we differed so radically [because] I [was] not one of your peace flock." Her disagreement with J.A. did not affect Mrs. Bowen's support of Hull House. Financial records kept by J.A. show that Mrs. Bowen donated $29,202.40 to Hull House in 1918—the most she had given in a single year since 1912.

Newspapers that had once sung J.A.'s praises now ran articles blasting her. Sometimes she was booed while presenting antiwar speeches, and several of her talks were canceled because of her pacifism. Harry Pratt Judson, the president of the University of Chicago, ridiculed her "so-called peace activities," adding that her antiwar talk was "giving aid and comfort to the enemy." Even many of her fellow social workers turned against her. About the time that the United States entered the war, Mary Simkhovitch of New York, the president of the National Federation of Settlements, announced that "it is very painful to many of us who hold Miss Addams in deep affection, to find that we cannot think or act in unison with her."

Most of the Hull House staff as well as the majority of neighborhood people disagreed with her, too. Hundreds of neighborhood men volunteered for military service and were shipped overseas, as were six of Hull House's male residents. Eleven members of the Hull House Band, along with their bandmaster, enlisted in the army and were sent into the war zone. In addition, a draft board was established for the Hull

FOUR DE PARIS IN THE ARGONNE ON THE LEFT AMERICAN LINES

J.A.'s nephew John Linn Jr. died on this field in France,
just before the end of the Great War.

House area, and longtime Hull House staff member George
Hooker, who had become one of the settlement's first male residents more than a quarter of a century earlier, was chosen to
run it.

Jane Addams did not try to stop these military activities so
close to home, for she knew that they reflected the will of the
majority. There was still worse news for her.

Many of J.A.'s own relatives supported the war. Her oldest
nephew, John Linn Jr., the son of her deceased sister Mary,
tried to enlist in the army even though he was a forty-six-year-
old Episcopalian minister with poor eyesight. He was turned
down because of his vision, but he managed to become a chap-
lain for an American artillery unit. Captain Linn spent the last
four months of his life at the battlefront. He regularly sent letters to the aunt who had been like a mother to him ever since
his own mother's death more than twenty years earlier. In his

final letter to his aunt Jane, the middle-aged minister expressed a premonition of his impending death. On October 8, 1918, as he moved along the foxholes passing out chocolate to the troops at the Battle of the Argonne in France, Captain John Linn Jr. was killed.

A month later, on November 11, 1918, the war ended in a victory for the Allies. It mattered little to Jane Addams that her reputation had been shattered by her opposition to the war. What troubled her most was that millions of people, including her dear nephew, had died—all because the leaders of the nations of the world hadn't found a peaceful way to settle their differences.

13

"The Most Dangerous Woman in America"

The world was still in shock after the war ended with the ceasefire agreement on November 11, 1918. No one had ever seen, and few people could have imagined, a war on such an enormous scale. Nearly 10 million soldiers and roughly an equal number of civilians had died, and approximately 21 million troops had been wounded. Many of the survivors were missing limbs and would never resume their former lives. Although physically unharmed, many other soldiers were suffering from shell shock (more often today called combat fatigue)—a dazed and confused condition that results from being under fire for long periods. To add to the misery, parts of Europe lay in ruin, leaving millions of people homeless and hungry.

The two most pressing needs, Jane Addams felt, were to aid the victims of the war and to make sure that a conflict like this never happened again. As president of the Woman's Peace

Party, which was the largest peace group for U.S. women, and of the Women's International League for Peace and Freedom, which was the world's leading female peace group, J.A. began working toward these goals.

In early 1919, representatives of the victorious Allies gathered in Paris, France, to frame the peace treaty that Germany would be forced to accept. The Women's International League for Peace and Freedom decided to hold a conference in Zurich, Switzerland, in the spring of 1919, at the same time that the peace treaty negotiations were taking place in Paris. But unlike the Paris conference, the women's convention would include representatives of the defeated as well as the victorious nations.

Her friends Florence Kelley and Dr. Alice Hamilton agreed to accompany J.A. to the Zurich conference. Not long before the journey to Zurich, Jane received word that her stepmother was critically ill. She took the train to Cedarville but arrived to find that Anna had lapsed into unconsciousness. Anna Haldeman Addams died a few weeks later, on April 23, 1919, at the age of ninety-two, while Jane was in Europe.

Addams, Hamilton, and Kelley sailed in early April of 1919 and arrived in France around the middle of the month. The women's conference wasn't scheduled to open in Zurich until May 12. J.A. arranged with the American Red Cross to use her extra time touring the war zone. She wanted to see the destruction for herself, and she hoped to find the grave of her nephew John.

For five days Jane Addams, Dr. Hamilton, and several other women were driven around France in two Red Cross vehicles.

Dr. Hamilton described their tour in a moving letter to her family:

Hotel Continental, Paris
May 1, 1919

Dear Family,

We came [here] last night after five days of motoring through the devastated regions and for almost all that time we hardly saw a town that was not devastated. We saw villages pounded to dust and great towns reduced to ruins and miles and miles of battle fields. One can't possibly imagine it, one has to see it and even then it is hard to believe. . . . I can't tell you how tragic it is, the villages especially. One feels that these humble little stone houses weren't the sort of thing that artillery ought to attack. It is like killing kittens with machine guns, they are so small and helpless. . . .

We went toward the Argonne . . . to hunt up John Linn's grave . . . and as we reached the farm where he is buried, our car sank deep in mud, and we climbed out and started off on foot. A muddy road [went] up over the ridge with desolate stretches on either side dug up to make the "fox holes" where the soldiers sheltered themselves. It was on his return from a trip to take food to the boys in their holes that the shell struck John. We found the graves in a hollow below the second

Dr. Alice Hamilton.
LIBRARY OF CONGRESS

ridge, down near a half ruined farm. There are
two rows of little crosses, about forty each. John's
is in between an Italian name and a Slavic
name. . . .

Jane Addams was too overcome by emotion to describe her
visit to her nephew's grave for her relatives in the States.
Dr. Hamilton closed her letter by asking her family to pass the
letter on to Jane Addams's niece Esther, John's sister.

From Paris, J.A. and her traveling companions continued on
to Zurich, where the Women's International League for Peace
and Freedom conference opened on May 12. Once again, the
remarkable aspect of this meeting was that women from both

sides came together in friendship. The women represented twenty-one nations, including Austria, Hungary, and Germany from the defeated countries, and Britain, France, Italy, Romania, and the United States from the victorious side.

During the six-day conference the women discussed ways to relieve hunger among European war victims. They condemned the peace treaty being hammered out in Paris, prophetically saying its harsh terms for Germany would "spread hatred" and "create animosities which can only lead to future wars." Most of them supported the creation of the League of Nations, an international organization of countries being established to maintain world peace. After the women resolved to hold another WILPF conference in two years, J.A. made a rousing closing speech on Saturday evening, May 17, 1919:

> So we can say to one another that we have met,
> and discovered that even after a great and
> prolonged war women from belligerent countries
> can come together, not in pretended good will,
> but in genuine friendship and understanding.
> If it can be done in small groups, then it can be
> done on a larger scale.

Following the Zurich conference, Miss Addams went back to Paris, where President Wilson was leading the American delegation at the peace talks. Through one of Wilson's advisers she relayed the resolutions from the recently completed WILPF conference to the president. However, there is no evidence that the final treaty was influenced by the women's opinions.

Herbert Hoover.

While abroad, J.A. was contacted by Herbert Hoover, an official who was leading American efforts to relieve hunger in Europe. Mr. Hoover, who had been appointed U.S. Food Administrator by President Wilson in 1917, involved Jane Addams and Dr. Alice Hamilton in a humanitarian project. The Quakers—a denomination that was staunchly antiwar—had raised $30,000 to feed hungry people in Germany. With

Mr. Hoover's assistance, the money was used to purchase thirty-five tons of condensed milk, ten tons of cocoa, and seventeen tons of sugar. J.A. and Dr. Hamilton were to accompany a committee of English and American Quakers that planned to distribute the food in Germany.

Addams and Hamilton arrived in Berlin, Germany, on July 7, 1919, just nine days after the peace treaty negotiated by the Allies was finally signed. Over the next few weeks the two American women visited children's hospitals and day nurseries in numerous German cities. They saw thousands of children who had nothing to eat but bread and watery "war soup," as they described in an article they wrote:

> In Leipzig we visited a large [child care center] in which 625 children from six to twelve years of age spend the day and are given a midday dinner. It consists of one pint of thin meal soup, to which had been added a little dried vegetable. Out of 190 children who were seated at one time in the dining room all except one were thin and anemic. What [doctors, nurses, and social workers] are facing is the shipwreck of a nation and they realize that if help does not come quickly and abundantly this generation in Germany is largely doomed to early death or a handicapped life.

J.A. sailed home in August 1919 and soon began speaking out about the need for food in Europe, including the defeated nations. She also campaigned to raise money for starving Ger-

HUNGER

For three years America has fought starvation *in* Belgium

Will you *Eat less* – wheat meat – fats *and* sugar that *we* may still send food *in* ship loads?

UNITED STATES FOOD ADMINISTRATION

This United States Food Administration poster urged Americans to eat less so that shiploads of food might be sent to starving children in Europe.

LIBRARY OF CONGRESS

man children. Even more so than during the war, she was bombarded with criticism by her countrymen, whose hatred for Germany and the other Central Powers hadn't been erased by the peace treaty. With more than 350,000 U.S. troops dead or wounded, few Americans were in the mood for Jane Addams's speeches about how we are all one human family, or her pronouncements that the best way to turn your enemies into your friends is to feed them.

Once again came cries of "traitor" from journalists and letter writers. When the nearly sixty-year-old J.A. spoke, she was often greeted by silence or boos. In Detroit, Michigan, the audience yelled at her for nearly an hour before allowing her to speak. In Cleveland, Ohio, a Red Cross worker blasted her speech as "an appeal for the mothers and babies of Germany and for their soldiers who had been wounded fighting our own boys." A man from Oak Park, Illinois, wrote J.A. a hate letter, saying, "If your 'mouthings' were not so ludicrous, they would be a stench in the nostrils of all decent people. Thank God, we are not afflicted with many citizens of your type."

Jane Addams wasn't attacked just for her pacifism. During the Great War, the Communist Revolution had taken place in Russia, which then became known as the Soviet Union. The Communists were called "Reds" because of the color of their flag. Despite the fact that Russia and the United States had been allies in the war, once the fighting ended, many Americans feared that the Russian Communists would infiltrate the United States and try to make it into a Communist country, too. America was swept by the "Red scare," a period when self-appointed "patriots" accused other Americans of being Communists or Communist sympathizers.

J.A. had encouraged people of many philosophies, including those with Communist leanings, to speak and hold meetings at Hull House. So in addition to taking abuse for being a pacifist (which she was) and for trying to help Germany recover from the war (which she did), she was also called a Communist (which she was not). After the war her name headed numerous lists of Americans accused of being Communists, including the "spiderweb charts" that were popular in the 1920s. By purporting to show how certain prominent people belonged to various "Communist-dominated" groups, these charts attempted to prove the existence of a widespread Communist conspiracy to take over the United States. A chart that a U.S. War Department librarian prepared in 1923 listed Jane Addams, Florence Kelley, and Julia Lathrop among the dangerous individuals, and the Women's International League for Peace and Freedom among the un-American organizations.

In 1919, President Wilson proclaimed November 11 as Armistice Day, to celebrate the anniversary of the ceasefire agreement that ended fighting in the Great War. Many speakers on this holiday—known today as Veterans Day—seized the opportunity to attack Jane Addams. Speaking at a 1926 Armistice Day program in Grand Rapids, Michigan, women's club official Mrs. Rufus C. Dawes warned her audience about peace groups "with communistic tendencies." Mrs. Dawes singled out WILPF as "unquestionably a very disloyal organization," adding that "Miss Addams herself does not conceal the fact that she does not believe in our own ideas of American loyalty."

Jane Addams became a special target of groups with military affiliations. Back in 1900, the Daughters of the American Revolution (DAR), an organization of women descended from patriots who helped win American independence, welcomed J.A. as a member. More than twenty years later, the DAR rescinded her membership and accused her of disloyalty to the United States. "All her actions have tended toward strengthening the hands of the Communists to make for the success of a Communist civil war in our country," read one DAR attack on Miss Addams.

The American Legion, an organization of military veterans, also doubted her patriotism. At an Armistice Day program in Chicago in 1926, Captain Ferre Watkins, commander of the Illinois American Legion, declared that "Hull House is the rallying point of every communistic movement in the country," and accused J.A. of aiding America's enemies by trying to strip the country of its weapons. But the most vicious attack on J.A. appeared in a publication of the Reserve Officers Training Corps (ROTC), which trains students to become officers in the nation's armed forces. For twenty years, declared the *Scabbard and Blade* in the late 1920s, Jane Addams had worked against her country's best interests "until today she stands out as the most dangerous woman in America."

Her friends rushed to J.A.'s defense. In July 1927, Carrie Chapman Catt published a letter defending her friend in the journal *Woman Citizen*. "The fact is that Miss Addams is one of the greatest women this republic of ours has produced," wrote Mrs. Catt. "She has given her life to serve others. She knows no selfish thought. You slap her on the right cheek, she only turns the left. Sticks, stones, slanders, you cast upon [her], and not a protest passes from her lips." Disgusted by the attacks, Florence Kelley wrote to J.A., also in July 1927: "I think the time has come when there must be a libel suit to stop this endless and ever more wide-spread sewage."

Though deeply wounded at being called disloyal to her country, "the most dangerous woman in America" had no intention of striking back at those trying to hurt her. After the DAR threw her out, J.A. tried to make light of it by saying she had thought her membership was for life—not just during good behavior. And in her personal files, she wrote a short note and attached it to a newspaper article in which Captain Ferre Watkins of the American Legion accused her of "attempting to sell out the country." Her note merely says "Captain Watkins Central 8140"—his telephone number. In keeping with her idea that communication was the key to making peace between individuals as well as nations, Addams evidently phoned Captain Watkins to discuss their differences.

By 1920, J.A. had concluded that another key to world peace was disarmament—the destruction of weapons so that countries couldn't fight a war even if they wanted to. Toward the end of 1920, she made a diary entry declaring the basic views that would guide her for the rest of her life:

> Believing that true peace can be secured only
> through reconciliation and good will and that
> no cause justifies the organized destruction of
> human life, I urge immediate and universal
> disarmament and promise never to aid in any
> way the prosecution of war.

Four years later, under Addams's direction, the Women's International League for Peace and Freedom clearly stated its main goal: "Complete and universal disarmament on land, on sea, and in the air." In other words, every country should voluntarily destroy its machine guns, bombs, fighter airplanes, battleships, submarines, and other tools of war.

Even many people who called themselves pacifists thought that this was just a pipe dream. It seemed virtually impossible that every nation on earth would agree to destroy all its weapons. In the unlikely event that such an agreement was made, what if one country broke its promise? That nation could then conquer all the others. Most advocates of disarmament felt that a nation should keep enough of its weapons to at least defend itself. In June 1925, J.A. responded to a friend who wanted to know what she meant by "complete disarmament":

> It seems to me that when we say "complete disarmament" we mean exactly what the physicians do when they say the abolition of tuberculosis. It may never be absolute but it is what we work towards.

Now in her sixties, Jane Addams traveled extensively to spread the word about disarmament. As WILPF president, she had presided over the conventions at The Hague in 1915 and Zurich in 1919. Over the next decade, J.A. continued to lead WILPF, presiding over its conventions in Vienna, Austria (1921), back at The Hague (1922), in Washington, D.C. (1924), Dublin, Ireland (1926), and Prague, Czechoslovakia (1929). She also made goodwill visits to many foreign lands to speak about peace.

One reason J.A. liked to travel overseas during the 1920s was that she was admired more abroad than she was at home. Branded a "Red" and "un-American" in the United States, she was viewed as a woman of noble ideas in other countries—the

The Peace Palace at The Hague.
LIBRARY OF CONGRESS

way her fellow Americans had once treated her. A more important reason she spent so much time abroad was that it gave her
hope. Meeting thousands of people from every corner of the
globe and discovering that they all wanted to live and raise their
families in peace made her optimistic about the future. Miss
Addams touched upon that subject in her presidential address at
the WILPF convention in Vienna in July 1921:

Although we are so near to the Great War with its millions of dead, we assert that war is not a natural activity for mankind, that it is very abnormal that large masses of mankind should fight against other large masses. We claim that mankind's natural tendency is to come into friendly relationship with ever larger groups.

We believe that the women of the world, realizing that war means the starvation of little children, will be roused to a sense of their age-long obligation to nurture children, to keep them alive. When [women] realize fully that war destroys everything that mothers have begun, there may be unleashed a tremendous force against war, a force more compelling than any[thing] which war propaganda can use in war's behalf.

Following the conference at The Hague in late 1922, Jane Addams embarked with Mary Rozet Smith on a nine-month trip around the world. During that time, J.A. met with public officials and spoke to large audiences in Burma, India, the Philippines, Korea, China, and Japan.

Miss Addams survived a couple of close calls on this lengthy trip. According to a letter Mary Rozet Smith wrote to Jane's niece Esther in mid-1923, J.A. had been riding in a two-wheeled cart called a rickshaw in Peking, China, when the vehicle overturned. Addams suffered a serious spill, severely bruising her arm and her side.

They went on to Japan, where Jane spoke to thousands of people in the city of Osaka on the subject "Women and Peace." She soon complained of feeling ill, and in Tokyo, the capital of Japan, she was taken to a hospital. J.A. hadn't broken any bones in the rickshaw accident, the doctors concluded, but they discovered a tumor on her right breast, which they removed without delay. J.A. recovered quickly, departing Japan in late August 1923 after three weeks of convalescence.

It turned out that Jane Addams and Mary Rozet Smith left Tokyo just in time. On September 1, 1923, a giant earthquake struck Japan. Falling buildings, fires, and huge sea waves called tsunamis killed more than 143,000 people, mostly in Tokyo and Yokohama.

Following further recuperation in Hawaii, J.A. returned to the States. A surprise awaited her when she arrived at Hull House on Sunday, September 23, 1923, two and a half weeks after her sixty-third birthday. Thousands of children were waiting to greet her outside the settlement house, which the staff had draped with "Welcome Home" decorations.

Whenever she was at Hull House, Addams spent much of her time corresponding with members of WILPF, which had its headquarters in Geneva, Switzerland. As mentioned earlier, she was president of the Woman's Peace Party, based in Chicago. She also served as an officer of at least seven other peace organizations headquartered in New York City, Washington, D.C., and Chicago. In addition, thirty other peace groups stayed in touch with J.A. to inform her of their activities or ask for her advice.

Although most of her efforts involved speaking and writing

against war, Addams occasionally took part in more spectacular antiwar protests. In December 1921, she presided over a mass peace meeting at an auditorium in Washington, D.C. Women from as far away as Russia, Japan, Sweden, and England attended this gathering. At the end of the proceedings, Jane Addams led the women on a twilight march through the streets of the U.S. capital to protest the lack of progress in disarmament among the world's powerful nations.

As she led the two-block-long procession past the White House, J.A. carried a banner that proclaimed THOU SHALL NOT KILL. Holding torches to light their way as well as signs asserting COMPLETE DISARMAMENT and NOT ONE SOLDIER, NOT ONE SAILOR, NOT ONE DOLLAR FOR WAR, the five hundred women then marched to other prominent landmarks in the nation's capital, attracting crowds of onlookers along the way.

The Women's International League for Peace and Freedom used the word "PAX" (meaning "peace" in Latin) as a motto. To call attention to WILPF, J.A. sometimes arranged for special trains called "PAX Specials" to take women to and from organization events. In the mid-1920s, J.A. also began to make guest appearances on a new medium—radio—to talk about peace.

As one of the world's leading pacifists, J.A. received hundreds of letters from people suggesting ways to establish peace. Some thought the answer was to have one flag for humanity rather than (or in addition to) separate flags for each nation. Their letters usually included their personal designs for a "World Flag" or "Peace Flag." On the other hand, Knut Sandstedt of Stockholm, Sweden, thought that language barriers

Mary McDowell (left) and seventy-two-year-old Jane Addams. An early resident of Hull House, McDowell later established the University of Chicago Settlement in 1894.

caused friction between countries. In 1920, he suggested to Miss Addams that English be adopted as the world language. Toys that taught children about fighting and war were the trouble, wrote Mary Elizabeth Baird Bryan of Miami, Florida, in 1923. Take away toy guns and other miniature weapons and children would grow up to be more peaceful, she insisted.

A real-estate agent in Richmond, Virginia, J. A. Connelly, believed that there were too many references to war in daily life. He was especially annoyed that the third month of the year was named for Mars, the Roman god of war. The name *March* should be changed to *Peace,* Mr. Connelly proposed in a 1928 letter to Jane Addams. Furthermore, the last Friday of the month of Peace should be an international holiday called Good Will Day. Zoe Evalyn Gregory, an attorney in Reno, Nevada, was convinced that differences in dress led to people not getting along. In a 1929 letter, Miss Gregory suggested that a contest be held to select a "world uniform."

Addams also received suggestions about schools for peace, peace awards, and peace prayers. Creative people sent her peace poems, peace music, and peace plays.

Yet for every American who agreed with J.A.'s crusade for peace, there were probably five who believed it was more important to be prepared for war. In their opinion, Jane Addams had done great things at Hull House, but she should "mind your own business," as one letter writer advised her, on matters of war and peace.

14

"A Mother for Everyone"

Dear J.A.," Julia Lathrop wrote in a 1930 letter, "No one else can manage much of anything on this planet as simply and effectively as you." At seventy, an age when many of her friends had retired, Jane Addams was still juggling three or four careers—and doing so quite well.

She remained the head resident and chief fundraiser for Hull House. When the settlement needed new boilers in 1925, J.A. raised the money. Each year she wrote pleas for donations for the Bowen Country Club, as the Hull House summer camp was called. It was difficult to resist her requests, such as her 1931 letter that began: "May we ask your help for a thousand children and many of their mothers, who, without your cooperation, will have to spend a dreary summer in the congested districts of Chicago?"

Addams also maintained a writing schedule that was a full-time job in itself. Between 1915 and 1930, she published four books: *Women at The Hague, The Long Road of Woman's Memory, Peace and Bread in Time of War,* and *The Second Twenty Years at Hull-House.* She continued to write articles, too, about war and

Little boys playing in a cart near Hull House, around 1930.
UNIVERSITY OF ILLINOIS, JANE ADDAMS MEMORIAL COLLECTION

peace, child labor, and education. One subject she didn't need
to write about much anymore was woman suffrage. Thanks to
the efforts of many people, including Jane Addams, in 1920 the
Nineteenth Amendment to the Constitution granted American
women the right to vote.

New generations of peace workers came along—people in their forties, thirties, and twenties—but Jane Addams was still the country's foremost female pacifist. A week rarely passed that she didn't write about disarmament, plan a WILPF convention, grant a newspaper interview, or speak about world peace. She especially enjoyed talking to students. "Take advantage of the opportunity to participate in the greatest movement of all time—world peace," she told an assembly of University of Arizona students on February 20, 1929. "Though peace advocates are accused of having their heads in the clouds, they are in reality among the ablest men and women of the age." Later that year, J.A. presided over the WILPF convention in Prague.

Having outlived all her brothers and sisters, J.A. was now the head of her family, which by the 1920s consisted of numerous nieces and nephews, grandnieces and grand-nephews, and great-grandnieces and great-grandnephews. She was a devoted aunt—making visits, sending Christmas and birthday gifts, writing cards and letters, and doing special things that let each relative know he or she had a special place in her heart.

When Marcet Haldeman fell in love, she wrote a thirty-two-page letter to J.A. that began: "Dearest Auntie, Emanuel Julius wants me to marry him and, unless you find some sound and strong reason against my doing so, I shall." Aunt Jane not only gave Marcet her blessing, she sent out the engagement announcements and apparently paid for the wedding. After Marcet and Emanuel Haldeman-Julius (they combined their last names) began a family, J.A. was like a grandmother to the children. In 1926, she sent a note to her grandniece Alice Haldeman-Julius:

> My dear Alice:
>   I am very pleased that you have asked me to sign your report card, and very proud indeed to sign one so full of E's and even E+'s. Sometime I hope to visit your school and see you actually at work.
>
>   Always your loving
>   Aunt Jane

Stanley Linn, who had been raised for a time at Hull House, could count on his Aunt Jane to bail him out of his frequent financial difficulties. In December 1916, J.A. sent Stanley two checks totaling $465.70 to help cover payments and repairs on his automobile. Stanley became a lemon grower in California, but when he and his wife, Myra, ran short of funds, J.A. sent them vacation money. On May 10, 1925, Stanley wrote J.A. a loving letter that began "Dear Aunt Jane—This is Mother's Day and you have been my 'Mother' for some thirty-four years, so I am writing to you."

Jane Addams sometimes took her young relatives on trips with her. In 1926, when she presided over the WILPF convention in Dublin, J.A. invited her grandniece Mary Addams Hulbert to accompany her to Europe. Upon learning of the invitation, Mary wrote, "Dear Aunt Jane: I can't really believe it is true. I never believed such a marvelous thing could happen to me! I have always been crazy to go to Europe!"

Back in the 1860s, young Jennie Addams had written OOOOO to represent hugs in her letters to family members. The tradition must have been handed down over the generations, because nearly sixty years later, in 1926, her great-grandnephew John Brittain did the same thing:

> Dear Great-Grand Aunt Jane,
>
> How are you? I am fine. I want to tell you how I luv my pink blanket. It keeps me nice and warm and my muther ses it maches my pink cheeks.
>
> I wish you wood cum and see me take my bath. Muther helps me but I can kick and splash myself.
>
> Here are sum kisses and hugs OOOOO
>
> > Lovingly yur
> >
> > grate grand nefew
> >
> > John

J.A. provided a wonderful treat for Stanley and Myra's daughter. At her grammar school in Arlington, California, the young girl boasted that her grandaunt was *the* Jane Addams mentioned in their history book. She had been named for her famous relative, who still lived in Chicago, Jane Addams Linn told her classmates. Jane Addams had to be dead, her friends insisted, because no one in a history book could still be alive. J.A. settled the argument by coming to speak at her grand-niece's school during a trip to California.

The most amazing aspect of J.A.'s busy schedule was that she accomplished so much despite no longer feeling well. After

An elderly Jane Addams surrounded by children.

many years of mostly good health, her age and weight began to catch up with her. In 1915, when she was fifty-five, she came down with pneumonia, and the following year she had to have a kidney removed. She underwent breast surgery in Japan in 1923, suffered a heart attack in 1926, and also was afflicted with a painful heart condition called angina.

Around 1929, J.A. had a pleasant change in her life. The brutal criticism and name-calling her fellow Americans had heaped on her because of her pacifism began to die down. More than a decade had passed since the end of the Great War—enough time to soften the hard feelings about her opposition to America's entry into the conflict. In addition, her dedication to the cause of peace year after year had gradually won her countrymen's respect. True, many people thought she had her "head in the clouds," as she said in her University of Arizona talk in early 1929. But how could anyone despise a woman who, despite failing health and advancing age, worked so hard to preserve life and find alternatives to war?

There was another reason Jane Addams's reputation made a comeback. The stock market crashed in October 1929. This began the Great Depression, a period of hard times and widespread unemployment that was to last over a decade. The jobless rate soared to ten, then twenty, then an astonishing twenty-five percent of the work force. Families lost their homes and farms. Children went hungry, and they couldn't attend school because they had no clothes to wear. In those days, before America had extensive government programs to help them, needy people depended on private agencies for assistance. Few people helped Depression victims as much as Jane Addams.

"I have watched fear grip the people in our neighborhood around Hull-House," J.A. wrote in 1931. "Men and women have seen their small savings disappear. Heads of families see hunger for their children—one of the most wretched things to endure." To ease the growing problem of poverty in her neighborhood, J.A. and her staff tried to find jobs for the unemployed. They also fed the hungry, as Louise deKoven Bowen recalled:

> There were times at Hull-House when Miss Addams and I did not know what to do with the crowds of unemployed. They came to us to ask for help. A woman who was to have a baby—where should she go? A man who had lost his leg—what could he do? A woman who had lost her breadwinner and was helpless. Hull-House tried then, as it has always tried, to give help to all these people.
>
> We called on the members of the Hull-House Women's Club, and using the little kitchen at Bowen Hall, very early Sunday mornings they made quantities of coffee and thousands of sandwiches.
>
> When all the [people] had gathered in the Hall, we had a little music, then we passed out sandwiches and coffee, so that they really had a very good meal. They could take as much coffee as they wanted and as many sandwiches as they could eat. I often saw a man put a sandwich in

his pocket, which I knew was to be given to a
wife or child.

Occasionally, J.A. was able to hire a neighborhood person to
work at Hull House as a cook or dishwasher. An unemployed
poet was put to work vacuum cleaning the settlement. He said
the job suited him because he could think out his poems while
he vacuumed. An ex-trapeze performer was hired to wash the

*Residents dining at Hull House. Jane Addams is seated at the end of the
table on the right.*
JANE ADDAMS HULL HOUSE ASSOCIATION, CHICAGO

windows at Hull House. "It was a pleasure to see him run along the sills and open and shut the windows on the third and fourth floors," Mrs. Bowen later recalled. Crowds of children, who didn't have a dime for a movie or a snack, came to Hull House to applaud the window washer as he went from window to window high above the ground.

Jane Addams's personal generosity won over most of her remaining critics. In the spring of 1931, Bryn Mawr College in Pennsylvania presented Addams with the M. Carey Thomas Prize, which awarded $5,000 "to an American woman in recognition of eminent achievement." That fall she won another $5,000 as part of the *Pictorial Review* award "to the woman who in her special field has made the most distinguished contribution to American life." Addams gave away the entire $10,000, which would be worth approximately $120,000 in today's money, to help impoverished people in the Hull House neighborhood.

Also in 1931, J.A. received the greatest honor of her life, but unfortunately, she was lying in a hospital bed at the time.

Late that year, after her seventy-first birthday, Jane Addams's health broke down completely. She suffered another heart attack. A growth, possibly cancerous, was found on her right ovary. J.A. checked into Johns Hopkins Hospital in Baltimore in early December to have the growth removed. While awaiting surgery, she received an important telegram: formal notice that she and Columbia University president Nicholas Murray Butler were co-winners of the 1931 Nobel Peace Prize. Issued in Oslo, Norway, this prestigious award is bestowed upon people who have performed great service on behalf of international peace.

Jane Addams with a young girl.
ROCKFORD COLLEGE, HOWARD COLMAN LIBRARY ARCHIVES

Since Addams was unable to attend the December 10 ceremony in Oslo, an American diplomat in Norway accepted the award for her. In presenting the Nobel Peace Prize, Professor Halvdan Koht of the University of Oslo said of Miss Addams:

Twice I have had the pleasure of visiting the institution where she has performed her life's work. In the slums of Chicago she has founded Hull House, where anyone desiring it may obtain aid. When one meets Jane Addams—in the assembly hall, the workroom, or the dining hall— one feels that here she has made a home, here is a mother for everyone. She is not one who talks much, but her quiet personality creates an atmosphere of good will.

Carrying on this social work amongst people of widely different nationalities, it was natural that she should take up the cause of peace, and for nearly twenty-five years she has been its faithful spokesman. She is the foremost woman of the nation. Therefore it meant so much that she worked for the cause of peace because so many millions of men and women looked up to her. She founded a big organization of women [to work for peace]. At times she had public opinion against her, but she did not give up and she won at last the place of honor she now holds.

Jane Addams almost did not live to read about this praise or to see her Nobel Peace Prize medal. At the time Professor Koht was making his speech in Oslo, J.A. was four thousand miles away preparing for surgery at Johns Hopkins. The operation to remove the ovarian growth was performed on December 12, 1931. According to James Weber Linn, his seventy-

Jane Addams (left) and Mary Rozet Smith.

one-year-old aunt lay near death for many hours during and after the operation because of a bad reaction to a new anesthetic. "Your Aunt Jane's operation [is] over and she [has] come through it very well," Mary Rozet Smith wrote to Stanley Linn the day after the surgery. "[But] they were quite alarmed during the operation as her blood pressure fell to an extremely low point and was not easily stimulated."

With Mary Rozet Smith keeping her company almost constantly, J.A. remained in the hospital another month. She was finally released on January 13, 1932, but she was too weak to resume normal activity. She and Mary went for a few weeks of rest and sun in Florida. Slowly J.A. gained strength, and on Saturday, March 26, 1932, the two dear friends arrived back in Chicago.

In addition to a beautiful medal and enormous prestige, the Nobel Peace Prize came with a very large cash award. Jane Addams's share of the prize amounted to $16,480.58—equivalent to about $200,000 in today's money. Everybody wondered: What would Jane Addams do with the money this time?

They soon found out. Addams had received the great prize in recognition of her work with the Women's International League for Peace and Freedom. So, in early 1932, she gave the bulk of the prize money—$15,000—to WILPF.

Many people, including some of her friends, considered the Nobel Peace Prize the crowning finish to Jane Addams's career. What was left for her to achieve? Her reputation had been restored at home. Abroad she was considered one of the greatest people America had ever produced. She had run the world's most famous settlement house for forty-three years.

She had worked tirelessly for peace, helped women win the right to vote, and written thought-provoking books. Now that her health was failing and she was headed toward her seventy-second birthday, she deserved to rest and let others take up the struggle against poverty and war.

Many people may have thought that, but Jane Addams wasn't one of them.

15

"The Heart That Beat for Humankind"

J.A. never fully regained her health following her late-1931 surgery. Her "funny old heart," as she called it, often gave her trouble, as did bronchitis. During periods when she was too ill to stay at Hull House, she was cared for at friends' homes—particularly the Chicago residences of Louise deKoven Bowen and Mary Rozet Smith.

The death of longtime friends was another blow that accompanied her old age. The year 1932 was an especially sad one for Jane. Florence Kelley died on February 17; two months later, on April 15, Julia Lathrop passed away. Of these three renowned social activists, only Jane Addams survived.

Ellen Gates Starr, who had helped J.A. establish Hull House forty-three years earlier, was still alive, but eight hundred miles away. Ellen had remained at the settlement house until 1920, when she had undergone spinal surgery that left her paralyzed below the waist. She had then gone to live at a

Seventy-year-old Jane Addams.

CEDARVILLE AREA HISTORICAL SOCIETY

Catholic convent in Suffern, New York. J.A. and Ellen exchanged letters, but in their later years they rarely saw each other.

As long as she could hold a pen, Jane Addams could still do meaningful work. In 1932, she published *The Excellent Becomes the Permanent,* a series of tributes to departed friends, many of whom had been pioneers of social work. Soon after, she began a new project that was close to her heart—a biography entitled *My Friend, Julia Lathrop.* J.A. also knew that many people were eager to read about *her* life, and she wanted them to get the facts straight. During the first half of the 1930s, she spent a great deal of time with her nephew James Weber Linn, who wrote an outstanding biography of her. She also assisted Winifred E. Wise, who wrote the only authorized children's biography of J.A. during her lifetime.

Meanwhile, it appeared that another major war might be brewing. In 1931, Japan invaded Manchuria, a region of China. Two years later, Nazi leader Adolf Hitler became chancellor of Germany. His country's defeat in the Great War would be avenged, Hitler boasted. With nations around the world preparing in case of another war, a number of people in every country, including Jane Addams in the United States, issued pleas for peace. Although she had resigned as the head of WILPF after the 1929 convention in Prague, J.A. remained the organization's "honorary president." As such, and as a Nobel Peace Prize winner, she continued to speak out against war in radio addresses and newspaper interviews.

On February 9, 1934, Jane Addams had another brush with death. "Your Aunt Jane had a very severe heart attack last

Friday evening at Hull-House and is still quite ill," Mary Rozet Smith explained in a letter to Stanley. "[Her doctors] insist on complete rest and seclusion."

Constant telephone calls and visitors would have made recovering at Hull House difficult, so J.A. went to the Chicago home of Mary Rozet Smith. While caring for her beloved friend, Mary neglected her own health. She developed pneumonia and sank quickly into a coma. On February 22, 1934, in a room just a few feet away from where Jane Addams was convalescing, Mary Rozet Smith took her last breath.

Her grief over Mary's death was so intense that for a while J.A. lost interest in life. "I suppose I could have willed my heart to stop beating, and I longed to do that," she told her nephew James, "but the thought of what she had been to me for so long kept me from being cowardly." Her doctors considered Jane Addams's condition too delicate for her to attend the memorial service, which was held in Mary's home. J.A. could only lie in her second-floor bedroom listening to the singing by the Hull House children's choir and the speeches by Mary's friends and relatives.

Cared for by friends, Jane Addams remained in Mary's home for another three months recovering from her heart attack and from her best friend's death. Much of the time she read. In fact, J.A. kept a written log of the books she read, much as she had nearly seventy years earlier when her father had paid her a nickel a book. J.A.'s list of "Books read during heart attack Feby. to May, 1934 12 West Walton Place" contains forty-two titles, ranging from murder mysteries to political works. Reading soothed her soul and relaxed her body. By

May 1934, she was ready to resume her life with the help of a cane.

J.A. accepted an invitation to join Dr. Alice Hamilton at her vacation home in Hadlyme, Connecticut, where, all summer, she worked on her biography of Julia Lathrop. Returning to Chicago in the fall, she moved in with Mrs. Bowen, who had installed an elevator to help J.A. move about her home. Her "funny old heart was behaving splendidly," J.A. soon announced. She felt so much better that she was able to work a few hours each day at Hull House.

Jane Addams spent the first few months of 1935 with Mrs. Bowen in Arizona, where she completed the first draft of her Julia Lathrop book. She also began planning yet another writing project. She made an outline for a book about the causes of war and placed it in an envelope labeled "J.A. Possible Idea for new book."

In April, she returned to Chicago, brimming with plans to revise the Julia Lathrop biography and begin the new project about the causes of war. But first there was an important event she was determined to attend.

The Women's International League for Peace and Freedom dated its founding from the spring of 1915, when the peace conference was held at The Hague. To celebrate WILPF's twentieth anniversary, a big gathering was scheduled in Washington, D.C., in early May 1935. Assuring her friends that she felt well enough to go, J.A. headed to Washington by train, where she arrived on May 1. She seems not to have realized that she was to be the center of attention at the festivities.

Her first day in the nation's capital, J.A. was whisked to a movie studio, where she was interviewed for a film newsreel. The next night, May 2, the twentieth-anniversary celebration was held in the ballroom of the Willard Hotel. More than a thousand people attended the dinner, and another five hundred came in afterward to hear the speeches, which were broadcast by national radio hookup.

Unless it was for the purpose of raising money for Hull House or the peace movement, J.A. had always discouraged testimonials in her honor. But there was no escaping this time, as speaker after speaker stood up before the audience and praised her accomplishments. Eleanor Roosevelt, the nation's First Lady, opened the program by saying: "It is for being yourself that I thank you tonight—and for the inspiration which your character and life have given to many people who have known of you, even if they have not had the opportunity of knowing you personally."

Secretary of the Interior Harold Ickes went next. "Jane Addams has dared to believe that the Declaration of Independence and the Constitution of the United States were written in good faith and that the rights declared in them are available to the humblest citizen," he said. "She is the truest American I have ever known, and there has been none braver. Parents who want to develop the finest in their children will bring them up in the Jane Addams tradition."

Labor leader Sidney Hillman declared, "Her life has been a beacon in the dark periods of our history, and she has been the center of some of the finest activities of the human spirit."

When all the speakers had finished singing her praises, J.A. was asked to respond. She could have graciously said "Thank you" for all the kind words. However, she wasn't about to pass up the chance to speak out for peace to an audience that included President Franklin D. Roosevelt's wife as well as thousands of radio listeners.

"We don't expect to change human nature, we people of peace," the gray-haired pacifist told her audience. "But we do hope to change human behavior. We may be a long way from permanent peace, and we may have a long journey ahead of us in educating the community and public opinion. It may not be an [easy task], but it tests our endurance and our moral enterprise, and we must see that we keep on doing it." What made her hopeful, she added, was that millions of people around the world felt that war was "unendurable," creating "a rising tide of revolt against war as an institution."

Over the next two days, J.A. took part in a historic event called the "Round-the-World Peace Broadcast." On the afternoon of May 3 and the morning of May 4, leaders from different parts of the globe spoke out over the radio for world peace. They sent out messages from London, Paris, Tokyo, Moscow, and Washington, D.C. In both the afternoon and morning broadcasts, Jane Addams, representing WILPF, was the final speaker.

"We find the messages of this wide-flung broadcast most exhilarating and encouraging," she told the radio audience. "The Women's International League joins a long procession of those who have endeavored for hundreds of years to substitute law for war, political processes for brute force."

The Round-the-World Peace Broadcast marked the last time Jane Addams would ever speak in public.

Early on the afternoon of May 4, J.A. boarded the train for Chicago, where she arrived the following day. The Washington trip seemed to have revitalized her. During the next ten days, she revised her Julia Lathrop biography and attended meetings to discuss the need for relief funds and better housing for Chicago's Depression victims.

At about two-forty-five on the morning of May 15, Jane Addams awoke in her room in Mrs. Bowen's house with an acute pain in her left side. She suffered all night in silence. When Mrs. Bowen entered the room at seven A.M. and found J.A. in pain, she asked her friend why she hadn't rung the emergency bell by her bed.

"I thought the bell was just in case I had a pain in my heart, and this was down one side," J.A. explained to Louise.

Over the next three days, Jane felt better, but her doctors suspected something serious and insisted that she undergo exploratory surgery without delay. When Louise deKoven Bowen tried to comfort her, J.A. assured her that she was not afraid to die because she had faith in an afterlife. "I want to know what it's going to be like," she told Louise.

On the morning of May 19, an ambulance was called to take Jane Addams to the hospital. Minutes before it arrived, Louise went into J.A.'s room and found her passing the time by reading. Sensing that Louise was extremely worried about her, Jane looked up from her book and said, "Don't look so solemn, dear."

At nine A.M., the ambulance arrived and took J.A. to Passavant Hospital, where she underwent surgery later that morning. The doctors discovered that she was suffering from incurable cancer. Jane Addams lived three days following the operation. Surrounded by relatives and friends, she died in her hospital bed at six-fifteen P.M. on Tuesday, May 21, 1935.

The death of seventy-four-year-old Jane Addams made headlines in virtually every newspaper in America, and in many other countries. Each paper had its own way of announcing the passing of this extraordinary human being. The Alton (Illinois) *Telegram* called her "A Big Great Soul," while to the Valley City (North Dakota) *Record* she was "an Apostle of Mercy to the poor and underprivileged." In San Francisco, California, the *Call-Bulletin* declared that "She Was Everybody's Friend."

Up in Hamilton, Ontario, Canada, the *Herald* announced, "Jane Addams, grand old lady, the world's greatest advocate for 'pacifism,' is dead." Down in El Paso, Texas, the *Post* stated that "With the passing of Jane Addams of Hull House the world loses one of its great women. Through all her 75 years, Miss Addams lived a life of passionate kindness. She hated injustice, cruelty, poverty, and, above all, war. But she loved people." Wanting its readers to remember her pacifism, the *Tribune* of Tampa, Florida, proclaimed: "Her life will ever stand as an example of consecrated service for human welfare and world peace."

At least one newspaper compared Jane Addams to her childhood hero. On May 23, 1935, the *News* of Los Angeles, California, published an editorial that began:

> Only with time can the stature of Jane Addams be measured. She has been styled "America's foremost woman citizen." She won the Nobel Prize.

She presided at the International Congress at The Hague and was honored by eminent societies in many countries.

When Abraham Lincoln died, her father told her, "the greatest man in the world has passed away." Little did the 5-year-old maid dream that 70 years later men and women in every land would say, when the news of her death was flashed along the cables, "the greatest woman in the world has passed away."

Chicago politicians were determined that no one would top *their* praise for *their* famous citizen. Ignoring the fact that Jane Addams had been a thorn in the side of many Windy City politicians over the years, the Chicago City Council passed a unanimous resolution calling her "the greatest woman who ever lived."

They may not have been able to express themselves as well as the newspaper writers, but people in cities and towns across America wanted to say what Jane Addams had meant to them, too. They sent poems and letters to Hull House by the hundreds. For example, a man in Yankton, South Dakota, named Will Chamberlain was moved to write a poem called "The Spirit of Jane Addams," which ended with the words:

> The heart that beat for humankind
> With never doubt or plod,
> Upon some other star may find
> New pulsings under God.

So while that form at Cedarville
In lonely vigil lies,
Jane Addams' soul is with us still
It never, never dies.

Many thousands of people came to honor Jane Addams at the service held for her at Hull House. At another service that was arranged by her old friend Flora Guiteau, Jane Addams was buried in the small cemetery near her birthplace in Cedarville, Illinois. This ceremony featured a group of students from the Cedarville school who stood waving American flags while singing "America the Beautiful."

Nothing could have been more fitting than the last words the children sang over Jane Addams:

America! America!
God shed His grace on thee,
And crown thy good with brotherhood
From sea to shining sea!

Afterword

◆

"To Plant the Seeds"

Following Jane Addams's death, Hull House continued to function under other directors for nearly thirty years. In 1963, most of the settlement's buildings were demolished to make way for the new Chicago campus of the University of Illinois. Two buildings that the wrecking ball spared were the original Hull House mansion and the dining hall. They were turned into the Jane Addams Hull-House Museum, which is operated by the University of Illinois at Chicago.

According to Louise deKoven Bowen, J.A. often said she hoped the day would come when Hull House and other settlements were no longer needed because the government had taken over all charitable work. Starting during the Great Depression, the government did become more involved in helping people. The year Jane Addams died—1935—the United States passed the Social Security Act. It established federal assistance programs for elderly people, needy children, and handicapped persons. Two years later, in 1937, the United States Housing Authority was founded to help poor people obtain decent housing. Other federal programs such

*This 1938 poster was created by an artist working with
the Federal Arts Project, a Depression-era government program.*

*More than a hundred years after Jane Addams opened the doors
of Hull House, these children play at a Hull House Association
community center.*

JANE ADDAMS HULL HOUSE ASSOCIATION, CHICAGO

as the Food Stamp Program and the Job Corps also offer the
kinds of assistance Hull House once provided.

But J.A. was wrong if she thought that settlement houses
would be completely replaced. There are still millions of
newcomers to America who need help learning English,

and huge numbers of adults who require assistance finding jobs and caring for their families. There are still many children who want to take part in sports, art, and music activities in their free time, and numerous men and women who want to attend night-school classes. Most communities have facilities that offer these kinds of services, only today they are rarely called "settlement houses." Instead they are known as "community centers," "community houses," or "neighborhood centers."

Jane Addams deserves some of the credit for the creation of these centers, for Hull House's success helped make them possible. And even though the Hull House settlement is gone, her dream of "the shelter we together build" still lives in Chicago. An organization called the Hull House Association runs approximately thirty community centers throughout the Windy City. These centers offer child care, family counseling, housing assistance, and other types of help to thousands of needy Chicagoans.

Today most of Jane Addams's reputation rests on her work at Hull House. Her peace efforts have largely been forgotten or ignored for decades. In fact, many people who consider Jane Addams a great woman feel uncomfortable when her crusade for peace is mentioned. That is because, at first glance, her efforts for peace seem to have been a dismal failure.

In 1939, just four years after J.A.'s death, another gigantic war began. This time Great Britain, Russia, China, France, the United States, and forty-five other Allies fought Germany, Japan, Italy, and several other Axis countries. By the time it ended in an Allied victory in 1945, the conflict had become the

This little girl is proud of her Hull House Association art project.
JANE ADDAMS HULL HOUSE ASSOCIATION, CHICAGO

deadliest war in world history. Approximately seventeen million men and women in uniform died in the war. The number of civilian deaths was far higher—in the tens of millions. This conflict was called World War II, while the clash that had been called the Great War was renamed World War I.

U.S. military strength was crucial to the Allied victory.

Had it not been brought to bear against Nazi Germany and the other Axis nations, they might have triumphed. In other words, had it disarmed, the United States along with many other nations might have been conquered by foreign dictatorships.

We decided to speak to several historians to find out how they view J.A.'s peace efforts. Seventy years after her death, we soon discovered, Jane Addams's pacifism is as controversial as it was in the early 1900s.

The Cedarville Historical Museum, 125 miles northwest of Chicago, has displays concerning the village's most famous citizen. There we spoke to Jim Bade, president of the Cedarville Area Historical Society, and to Ronald Beam, a local historian and former president of the society.

"I think her Hull House work was more important than her peace work," Mr. Bade told us, "because it accomplished social changes and cleaned up part of Chicago. She didn't accomplish what she wanted in regard to war. I think her peace work was a pipe dream. We've been pursuing peace since Cain and Abel. After a war, we always say, 'We'll never let that happen again,' but it does."

Ronald Beam agreed. "In regard to her peace work, I think the world would call her a little bit naive," said Mr. Beam, implying that Jane Addams was innocent and a bit foolish. "She was antiwar—what we would call a peacenik today. She opposed our participation in World War I, and she would have fought tooth and nail for us to stay out of World War II, the Vietnam War, and the Iraq War. She had a desire for peace that came from goodheartedness and wishful thinking, but the reality is that you have evil men in this world who have agendas that won't be negotiated."

Other historians think that J.A. achieved a great deal with her antiwar efforts. "Addams was a pioneer of peace," said Narcissa Engle, vice president of the Cedarville Area Historical Society. "By placing her reputation on the line, she helped the tree of peace to grow for people yet unborn."

Chris Gordy is the executive director of the Stephenson County Historical Society, located a few miles from Cedarville in Freeport, Illinois. "Jane Addams didn't fail in her peace work," Mr. Gordy insisted. "I don't call the fact that she couldn't stop World War I a failure. Her purpose was to change people's notions about peace and to plant the seeds of world peace in people's minds."

If viewed as a seed planter, Jane Addams can be credited with helping to end a later conflict. She and her fellow pacifists from the World War I era helped establish a tradition of protest against America's involvement in wars. One conflict in which a later generation of protesters achieved noteworthy success was the Vietnam War. Thanks partly to demonstrations and protests by hundreds of thousands of Americans, the United States pulled out of the Vietnam War in 1973 after nearly ten years of involvement. Had she still been alive in the 1960s, J.A. undoubtedly would have marched shoulder to shoulder with the Vietnam War protesters. And if she could come back in 2006, is there any doubt that she would organize protests against the war in Iraq?

Of course, the ultimate goal of pacifists is to prevent wars from starting in the first place. We are a long way from that goal, and many people are convinced that we will never achieve it. But with her boundless optimism about human beings, J.A. believed that world peace is within our grasp.

Perhaps Jane Addams put it best when she spoke at the twentieth-anniversary celebration of the Women's International League for Peace and Freedom just nineteen days before her death:

> We may be a long way from permanent peace,
> and we may have a long journey ahead of us in
> educating the community and public opinion.
> It may not be an [easy task], but it tests our
> endurance and our moral enterprise, and we
> must see that we keep on doing it.

The United States Postal Service issued the Jane Addams postage stamp in 1940.

UNIVERSITY OF ILLINOIS, JANE ADDAMS MEMORIAL COLLECTION

Source Notes

Jane Addams is abbreviated as J.A.

The Jane Addams Papers are abbreviated as TJAP.

J.A.'s autobiography *Twenty Years at Hull-House* is referred to as *Twenty*.

Jane Addams: A Biography by James Weber Linn is abbreviated as *JA-Linn*.

Full bibliographic information appears in the Bibliography, beginning on page 210.

INTRODUCTION

p. vii   The nicknames "Angel of Democracy," "Lady of God," and "Saint Jane" are mentioned on pages 427, 259, and 433, respectively, in *JA-Linn*; the "Miss Kind Heart" nickname appears on page 72 of *With One Bold Act* by Barbara Garland Polikoff.

p. viii   The "most dangerous woman in America" quote appears on page 267 of *American Heroine* by Allen F. Davis.

p. viii   J.A. describes herself as "absolutely at sea" on page 68 of *Twenty*.

p. viii   Politician Johnny Powers is said to have called J.A. "a saint from the skies" on page 455 of *City of the Century* by Donald L. Miller.

CHAPTER 1: MISS ADDAMS, GARBAGE INSPECTOR

Much of the information about J.A.'s stint as Nineteenth Ward Garbage Inspector comes from pages 152–55 of *Twenty*.

p. 1   The statistic that half of Chicago's children died before the age of five in the late 1880s appears on page 140 of *A Useful Woman* by Gioia Diliberto.

p. 5   The "careful inspection" quote appears on page 155 of *Twenty*.

CHAPTER 2: LAURA JANE ADDAMS, "UGLY DUCKLING"

The main sources for this chapter are *Twenty* and *JA-Linn*.

pp. 7–8   The story of Sarah Addams's death is told on page 22 of *JA-Linn*.

pp. 9–10   The life of John Addams, J.A.'s father, is discussed on pages 7–8 of *Cedarville's Jane Addams* by Ronald H. Beam and also on pages 1–21 of *JA-Linn*.

p. 10   Jim Bade discussed John Addams's support for Abraham Lincoln during a 2005 interview with the authors in Cedarville.

p. 10   The "MR. LINCOLN'S LETTERS" story is told on page 38 of *JA-Linn*.

p. 11   J.A. tells about her father paying her to read on page 61 of *Twenty*, and additional information is on page 37 of JA-Linn.

pp. 11–12   The story of the couple who lost four sons in the Civil War and their last son in a hunting accident is on pages 51–52 of *Twenty*.

p. 13   J.A. describes her nightmare about the wagon wheel and her visits to the blacksmith's shop on pages 43–44 of *Twenty*.

p. 13   J.A.'s "ugly duckling" comment appears on page 45 of *Twenty*.

p. 14   J.A.'s "I imagined" quote about her feeling ugly as a child appears on pages 44–45 of *Twenty*.

p. 14   The story of John Addams tipping his hat and bowing to young J.A. appears on page 45 of *Twenty*.

CHAPTER 3: "JENNIE AND GEORGIE"

p. 15   Anna Haldeman Addams, J.A.'s stepmother, is described on pages 10–11 of *Cedarville's Jane Addams* and on pages 45–50 of *A Useful Woman* by Gioia Diliberto.

p. 17   J.A. and Georgie's childhood activities are chronicled on pages 11, 15, and 16 of *Cedarville's Jane Addams* and more extensively in *Jane Addams of Hull-House* by Winifred E. Wise.

pp. 18–19   Georgie and J.A.'s owl's nest exploit is related in *Jane Addams of Hull-House* on pages 35–36.

p. 21   The family trip to see the eagle Old Abe is related on page 52 of *Twenty*.

p. 21   J.A.'s and Georgie's pictures are in TJAP.

p. 21   J.A.'s joke book *Pepper and Salt* is at the Cedarville Area Historical Society.

p. 24   J.A.'s January 14, 1872, letter to her sister Alice is from TJAP.

pp. 25–26   The 1875 J.A. diary entries are from TJAP.

pp. 27–28   The story about J.A. seeing the tumbledown shanties and then predicting that she would one day live among the poor appears on page 52 of *A Useful Woman* and on page 27 of *JA-Linn*.

CHAPTER 4: JANE ADDAMS, COLLEGE GRADUATE

p. 31   Eleanor Frothingham Haworth's quote about first meeting J.A. appears on pages 40–41 of *JA-Linn*.

p. 32   Miss Sill's statement about the seminary's purpose comes from TJAP.

p. 34   The story about the teacher hiding when she heard Miss Sill coming appears on page 22 in Margaret Roherty Sedeen's chapter entitled "Anna Peck Sill: Visible Saint" in *A Power Not of the Present*.

p. 34   The "firm Sill" riddle appears on page 27 of "Anna Peck Sill."

pp. 34–35   The quote about J.A. sparkling with enthusiasm while at Rockford Female Seminary appears on page 46 of *JA*-Linn.

p. 35   The letter from Rollin Salisbury inviting J.A. to a scientific lecture is in TJAP.

p. 35   A reference to Rollin Salisbury's marriage proposal to J.A. is on page 50 of *JA*-Linn.

p. 36   The *Don Quixote* story and J.A.'s poem appear on page 48 of *JA*-Linn.

p. 38   J.A.'s "Always do what you are afraid to do" motto is in TJAP.

pp. 38–39   J.A. admits that she once abused the drug opium on page 60 of *Twenty*.

p. 39   J.A.'s classes and grades at the seminary come from TJAP.

p. 39   J.A.'s article "Follow Thou Thy Star" is in TJAP.

p. 40   The "Do what you believe in doing" quote is on page 62 of *JA*-Linn.

p. 41   J.A.'s graduation speech appears in TJAP.

CHAPTER 5: "ABSOLUTELY AT SEA"

pp. 42–43   J.A. describes feeling lost following her graduation from Rockford Female Seminary on page 68 of *Twenty*.

p. 44   John Addams's death is related on pages 65–66 of *JA*-Linn.

pp. 46–47   J.A.'s experiences at the Women's Medical College of Philadelphia and at the Mitchell Hospital are related on pages 84–94 of *A Useful Woman* by Gioia Diliberto.

p. 48   Dr. Harry Haldeman's operation on his stepsister J.A. is discussed on page 178 of *JA*-Linn.

CHAPTER 6: "I WOULD BEGIN TO CARRY OUT THE PLAN"

pp. 51–56   J.A. described her European experiences on pages 68–74 of *Twenty*.

pp. 56–57   J.A.'s volunteer work in Baltimore is related on page 118 of *A Useful Woman* by Gioia Diliberto.

p. 58   Several of J.A.'s letters in TJAP describe her experience at the bullfight.

pp. 58–59   J.A.'s comment that she would "begin to carry out the plan" comes from pages 77–78 of *Twenty*.

p. 59   J.A.'s Toynbee Hall visit is described on pages 53–54 of *With One Bold Act* by Barbara Garland Polikoff and on page 131 of *A Useful Woman*.

Chapter 7: "The Shelter We Together Build"

pp. 60–67 Chicago history and the conditions in the city are described in Donald L. Miller's *City of the Century* and in *City of Big Shoulders* by Robert G. Spinney.

p. 68 J.A. calls Hull House "a fine old house" on page 80 of *Twenty*.

pp. 68–69 Conditions in the Nineteenth Ward are discussed on page 151 of *A Useful Woman* by Gioia Diliberto.

pp. 70–71 J.A. describes moving into Hull House on page 81 of *Twenty*.

p. 71 J.A.'s "A house stands on a busy street" poem is in TJAP.

Chapter 8: "A Sense of Fellowship"

p. 72 J.A. wrote of the "honesty and kindliness of our new neighbors" on page 81 of *Twenty*.

p. 72 The stone-throwing incident is described on pages 157–58 of *A Useful Woman* by Gioia Diliberto.

pp. 72–73 Hull House's early days are chronicled on pages 67–69 of Allen F. Davis's *American Heroine*, on pages 158–68 of *A Useful Woman*, and on various pages of *Twenty*.

pp. 75–76 Florence Kelley's description of her arrival at Hull House appears on pages 38–39 of *Jane Addams and the Dream of American Democracy* by Jean Bethke Elshtain.

p. 77 The classes Hull House offered are described in TJAP.

pp. 78–79 The Illinois Factory Act of 1893 is described on page 123 of *Twenty* and on page 178 of *A Useful Woman*.

pp. 79–85 Various parts of *Twenty* describe the growth of Hull House.

Chapter 9: "Miss Kind Heart"

pp. 86–87 J.A.'s efforts on behalf of the Linn children are discussed on pages 213–14 of *A Useful Woman* by Gioia Diliberto.

pp. 87–88 The attempted burglaries are described on page 114 of *JA-Linn*.

pp. 88–90 Alderman Johnny Powers's career is discussed on pages 453–55 of *City of the Century* by Donald L. Miller.

pp. 90–91 The incident in which Powers blocked construction of a new school is described on pages 121–22 of *American Heroine* by Allen F. Davis.

pp. 90–94 J.A.'s political battles with Johnny Powers are described on pages 122–25 of *American Heroine*.

p. 93 The letter from "A Voter" is in TJAP.

p. 95   The August 10, 1909, *New York Evening Post* editorial promoting J.A. as a presidential candidate is quoted on page 299 of *Jane Addams and the Dream of American Democracy* by Jean Bethke Elshtain.

p. 97   The occasion when J.A. and Julia Lathrop assisted with a birth is described on pages 92–93 of *Jane Addams and the Dream of American Democracy*.

pp. 98–99   The Hilda Satt Polacheck quotes come from pages 30, 51–52, and 75 of her book, *I Came a Stranger*.

p. 100   The letter young Samuel Soleycocks wrote from jail is in TJAP.

CHAPTER 10: "LET ME HOLD YOUR FOOT"

Much of the information in this chapter comes from Louise deKoven Bowen's *Open Windows*.

p. 101   The "Let me hold your foot" story is related on pages 226–27 of *Open Windows*.

p. 102   A description of how J.A. relaxed by redecorating Hull House is on pages 252–53 of *Open Windows*.

pp. 102–3   The March 14, 1894, letter to Mrs. McCormick is in TJAP.

pp. 103–4   J.A.'s correspondence with Helen Culver is in TJAP.

pp. 104–6   The stories of J.A. giving away her clothing come from pages 219–20 of *Open Windows*.

pp. 106–7   A description of how J.A. pretended to speak to one person in an audience is on page 118 of *JA-Linn*.

p. 107   The elevator story appears on page 226 of *Open Windows*.

p. 107   J.A.'s habit of wearing rubbers over her shoes is recounted on pages 221–22 of *Open Windows*.

p. 108   The conversation with the receptionist about J.A.'s slip showing comes from page 222 of *Open Windows*.

pp. 108–9   The Abraham Isaak story is on pages 191–94 of *Twenty*.

pp. 109–10   Dan Portincaso told the authors about J.A. and the 1919 race riot when we interviewed him in 2004.

p. 110   During the same interview, Dan Portincaso told the authors about Anna Haldeman Addams never visiting Hull House.

p. 111   J.A.'s March 15, 1910, letter to her stepmother is in TJAP, as are the letters J.A. wrote in the hospital during her grandnephew's surgery and J.A.'s correspondence with Flora Guiteau.

p. 112   Dan Portincaso told the authors in 2004 about J.A.'s close relationship with Mary Rozet Smith's parents.

p. 113   The December 1896 letter from Mary Rozet Smith to J.A. is in TJAP.

p. 114 Donald L. Miller asserts that J.A. and Mary Rozet Smith were "quite likely lovers" on page 420 of *City of the Century*.

p. 114 Jean Bethke Elshtain's comment about women sharing "love, friendship, and joy" is on page 117 of *Jane Addams and the Dream of American Democracy*.

pp. 114–15 J.A.'s religious views are discussed on page 269 of *Open Windows*.

CHAPTER 11: "BECAUSE OF WHAT YOU ARE AND STAND FOR"

Much of the information for this chapter comes from TJAP.

pp. 117–18 The comparison of J.A.'s writing style to quilting appears on page 95 of Barbara Garland Polikoff's *With One Bold Act*.

pp. 118–19 Documents relating to J.A.'s NAACP work are in TJAP.

p. 120 J.A.'s article "If Men Were Seeking the Franchise" is reprinted on pages 232–38 of *Twenty*.

p. 120 J.A.'s appearance in the silent movie is described on page 198 of *American Heroine* by Allen F. Davis and on page 261 of *A Useful Woman* by Gioia Diliberto.

p. 121 Theodore Roosevelt's visits to Hull House are recounted in TJAP.

pp. 121–24 TJAP provided material relating to J.A.'s participation in Theodore Roosevelt's presidential campaign, including her seconding speech, T.R.'s thank-you that followed, the campaign songs, and J.A.'s speaking schedule on behalf of T.R.

CHAPTER 12: "THE CAUSE OF PEACE"

The bulk of the information for this chapter comes from TJAP.

p. 126 The thousand tourists a day Hull House attracted one summer, and the story of the tour guide who thought J.A. had died, are mentioned on pages 248–49 of *Open Windows* by Louise deKoven Bowen.

p. 129 J.A.'s letter informing Carrie Chapman Catt of her dedication to "the cause of peace" as well as J.A.'s and Mrs. Catt's correspondence regarding the peace meeting come from TJAP.

pp. 130–31 J.A.'s speech to the Woman's Peace Party and the preamble to the Peace Platform are from TJAP.

p. 132 Information about the illnesses and deaths of J.A.'s relatives is in TJAP.

pp. 132–33 J.A.'s March 26, 1915, letter to Lillian Wald is in TJAP.

p. 133 The ocean crossing aboard the Noordam is described on pages 300–302 of *JA-Linn*.

p. 135 J.A.'s presidential address and other information about the origins of WILPF come from TJAP.

pp. 136–37 J.A.'s meetings with European leaders are described on pages 306–7 of *JA*-Linn.

p. 138 J.A.'s correspondence with Henry and Clara Ford is in TJAP.

pp. 138–40 J.A.'s January 13, 1916, testimony before the U.S. House of Representatives Committee on Military Affairs is in TJAP.

pp. 140–44 The letters to J.A. from Lucy K. Kellogg, from "a mother of sons," and from the elderly man in Kirkwood, Illinois, as well as the April 16, 1917, letter from J.A. and other pacifists to President Woodrow Wilson, are in TJAP.

p. 144 Ex-president Theodore Roosevelt's insulting comments about J.A.'s peace efforts, including his reference to her as a "Bull Mouse," come from page 223 of *American Heroine* by Allen F. Davis.

p. 145 Mrs. Bowen's letter recalling how she disagreed with J.A. during World War I is in TJAP.

p. 145 Harry Pratt Judson's comments about J.A.'s "so-called peace activities" appear on pages 233–34 of Jean Bethke Elshtain's *Jane Addams and the Dream of American Democracy*.

p. 145 Mary Simkhovitch's remarks criticizing J.A. appear on pages 330–31 of *JA*-Linn.

pp. 146–47 The war experiences and death of Captain John Linn Jr. are related on page 185 of *With One Bold Act* by Barbara Garland Pollkoff.

CHAPTER 13: "THE MOST DANGEROUS WOMAN IN AMERICA"

TJAP provided most of the material for this chapter.

pp. 149–52 Information about the WILPF conference in Zurich, including the text of J.A.'s closing speech, comes from TJAP, as does Dr. Alice Hamilton's letter about the destruction in Europe and the search for the grave of Captain John Linn Jr.

pp. 153–54 J.A.'s contact with Herbert Hoover and her description of seeing starving children in Germany come from pages 259–60 of *American Heroine* by Allen F. Davis.

p. 156 The booing that J.A. received in Detroit and the criticism from the Red Cross worker in Cleveland are described on page 260 of *American Heroine*.

p. 156 The hate letter from the man in Oak Park, Illinois, is in TJAP.

pp. 156–58 The "spiderweb charts" are described on pages 263–64 of *American Heroine,* and the DAR attack on J.A. is on page 267 of the same book.

pp. 157, 158   Mrs. Rufus C. Dawes's accusations against J.A. are in TJAP, as is the attack by Captain Ferre Watkins.

p. 158 The "most dangerous woman in America" accusation appears on page 267 of *American Heroine.*

pp. 158–59 Carrie Chapman Catt's "greatest women" letter is in TJAP, as is Florence Kelley's "wide-spread sewage" letter and J.A.'s scrap of paper with Captain Watkins's phone number.

pp. 159–60 J.A.'s diary entry vowing "never to aid in any way the prosecution of war" is from TJAP, as are WILPF's declaration of "complete and universal disarmament" and J.A.'s explanation of what was meant by "complete disarmament."

pp. 161–62 J.A.'s 1921 presidential address at the WILPF convention in Vienna is in TJAP.

p. 162 J.A.'s rickshaw accident in China and her breast surgery in Japan are chronicled in TJAP.

p. 164 Letters J.A. received from peace activists and peace groups around the world are in TJAP.

p. 164 Information about the 1921 peace march and the "PAX Special" trains comes from TJAP.

pp. 164–66 Hundreds of letters suggesting ways to establish peace as well as letters ridiculing J.A.'s peace activities are in TJAP.

CHAPTER 14: "A MOTHER FOR EVERYONE"

p. 167 Julia Lathrop's 1930 "Dear J.A." letter and J.A.'s 1931 plea for donations both come from TJAP.

p. 169 J.A.'s "world peace" speech to the University of Arizona students is in TJAP.

pp. 169–71 J.A.'s correspondence with Marcet Haldeman-Julius, Alice Haldeman-Julius, Stanley Linn, Mary Addams Hulbert, John Brittain, Jane Addams Linn, and many other relatives is in TJAP.

p. 174 J.A.'s "I have watched fear grip the people" statement appears on page 287 of *American Heroine* by Allen F. Davis.

pp. 174–75 Louise deKoven Bowen's recollections of feeding the hungry at Hull House appear on pages 235–36 of *Open Windows* by Louise deKoven Bowen.

pp. 175–76 The unemployed poet and the ex-trapeze performer who went to work at Hull House are described on pages 236–37 of *Open Windows.*

p. 176 Information about the M. Carey Thomas and the *Pictorial Review* prizes comes from TJAP; *American Heroine,* page 286, describes how J.A. gave away the $10,000 prize money.

pp. 176–80 Information about the Nobel Peace Prize, including Professor Koht's speech and details about J.A. giving most of the money to WILPF, comes from TJAP.

p. 178 J.A.'s surgery is described in TJAP and on page 392 of *JA*-Linn.

CHAPTER 15: "THE HEART THAT BEAT FOR HUMANKIND"

Most of the material for this chapter was provided by TJAP.

p. 182 The "funny old heart" expression is mentioned on page 408 of *JA*-Linn.

pp. 184–85 Mary Rozet Smith's letter about JA's February 9, 1934, heart attack is in TJAP.

p. 185 J.A.'s comment about willing her "heart to stop beating" appears on pages 407–8 of JA-Linn.

p. 185 J.A.'s written log of books she read while recovering from her heart attack is in TJAP.

p. 186 J.A.'s notes for her planned "new book" are in TJAP.

pp. 186–88 The information for WILPF's twentieth-anniversary celebration, including the "Round-the-World Peace Broadcast," comes from TJAP.

p. 189 J.A.'s illness at Mrs. Bowen's house is described on page 271 of *Open Windows,* on pages 419–20 of JA-Linn, and in TJAP.

pp. 189–90 Information about J.A.'s final surgery and death, as well as the newspaper tributes, poem, and descriptions of her memorial services, all come from TJAP.

AFTERWORD: "TO PLANT THE SEEDS"

p. 193 J.A.'s remarks that she looked forward to the day when settlements were no longer needed appear on page 262 of *Open Windows* by Louise deKoven Bowen.

pp. 198–99 The authors interviewed Jim Bade, Ronald Beam, and Narcissa Engle in Cedarville in 2004 and 2005.

p. 199 The authors interviewed Chris Gordy in Freeport in 2005.

p. 200 J.A.'s "We may be a long way from permanent peace" speech comes from TJAP.

Bibliography

COLLECTION OF DOCUMENTS

The Jane Addams Papers (82 reels), Mary Lynn McCree Bryan, editor. Ann Arbor, Michigan: University Microfilms International, 1984.

BOOKS

Addams, Jane. *My Friend, Julia Lathrop*. New York: Macmillan, 1935.

——. *The Second Twenty Years at Hull-House, September 1909 to September 1929*. New York: Macmillan, 1930.

——. *Twenty Years at Hull-House: With Autobiographical Notes*. Boston: Bedford/St. Martin's, 1999 (originally published in 1910).

Beam, Ronald H. *Cedarville's Jane Addams . . . Her Early Influences*. Freeport, Illinois: Wagner, 1966.

Bowen, Louise deKoven. *Open Windows: Stories of People and Places*. Chicago: Seymour, 1946.

Davis, Allen F. *American Heroine: The Life and Legend of Jane Addams*. New York: Oxford University Press, 1973.

Diliberto, Gioia. *A Useful Woman: The Early Life of Jane Addams*. New York: Scribner, 1999.

Elshtain, Jean Bethke. *Jane Addams and the Dream of American Democracy: A Life*. New York: Basic Books, 2002.

Knight, Louise W. *Citizen: Jane Addams and the Struggle for Democracy*. Chicago: University of Chicago Press, 2005.

Levine, Daniel. *Jane Addams and the Liberal Tradition*. Madison, Wisconsin: State Historical Society of Wisconsin, 1971.

Linn, James Weber. *Jane Addams: A Biography*. New York: Appleton-Century, 1935.

Mackevich, Eileen, Gene W. Ruoff, and Linda Vavra, project directors. *Jane Addams' Hull-House*. Chicago: University of Illinois at Chicago, 1989.

Miller, Donald L. *City of the Century: The Epic of Chicago and the Making of America*. New York: Simon & Schuster, 1996.

Polacheck, Hilda Satt. *I Came a Stranger: The Story of a Hull-House Girl*. Urbana, Illinois: University of Illinois Press, 1989.

Polikoff, Barbara Garland. *With One Bold Act: The Story of Jane Addams*. Chicago: Boswell, 1999.

Sedeen, Margaret Roherty. "Anna Peck Sill: Visible Saint" from *A Power Not of the Present*. Asprooth, Elizabeth M., editor. Rockford, Illinois: Rockford College Press, 1973.

Spinney, Robert G. *City of Big Shoulders: A History of Chicago*. DeKalb, Illinois: Northern Illinois University Press, 2000.

Wise, Winifred E. *Jane Addams of Hull-House: A Biography*. New York: Harcourt, Brace, 1935.

Index

Note: Page numbers in **bold** type refer to illustrations.